InterActions
small group series

Clear
Answers to
Confusing
Issues

BIG
QUESTIONS

Interactions Small Group Series

Authenticity: Being Honest with God and Others
Big Questions: Clear Answers to Confusing Issues
Celebrating God: Discover the Truth of God's Character
Character: Reclaiming Six Endangered Qualities
Commitment: Developing Deeper Devotion to Christ
Community: Building Relationships within God's Family
Essential Christianity: Practical Steps for Spiritual Growth
Excellent Living: Giving God Your Best
Fruit of the Spirit: Living the Supernatural Life
Getting a Grip: Finding Balance in Your Daily Life
Influence: Maximizing Your Impact for God
Jesus: Seeing Him More Clearly
Lessons on Love: Building Deeper Relationships
Living in God's Power: Finding God's Strength for Life's Challenges
Love in Action: Experiencing the Joy of Serving
Marriage: Building Real Intimacy
Meeting God: Psalms for the Highs and Lows of Life
New Identity: Discovering Who You Are in Christ
Parenting: How to Raise Spiritually Healthy Kids
Prayer: Opening Your Heart to God
Reaching Out: Sharing God's Love Naturally
The Real Deal: Discover the Rewards of Authentic Relationships
Significance: Understanding God's Purpose for Your Life
Transformation: Letting God Change You from the Inside Out

InterActions
small group series

Clear
Answers to
Confusing
Issues

BIG
QUESTIONS

BILL HYBELS

WITH KEVIN AND SHERRY HARNEY

ZONDERVAN®   WILLOW
                     Willow Creek Resources

ZONDERVAN.com/
AUTHORTRACKER
follow your favorite authors

ZONDERVAN

Big Questions
Copyright © 2010 by Willow Creek Association

Requests for information should be addressed to:

Zondervan, *Grand Rapids, Michigan 49530*

ISBN 978-0-310-28065-1

Interior design by Rick Devon and Michelle Espinoza

Printed in the United States of America

09 10 11 12 13 14 15 16 17 18 • 20 19 18 17 16 15 14 13 12 11 10 9 8 7 6 5 4 3 2 1

CONTENTS

INTERACTIONS

In 1992, Willow Creek Community Church, in partnership with Zondervan and the Willow Creek Association, released a curriculum for small groups entitled the Walking with God series. In just three years, almost a half million copies of these small group study guides were being used in churches around the world. The phenomenal response to this curriculum affirmed the need for relevant and biblical small group materials.

At the writing of this curriculum, there were nearly 3,000 small groups meeting regularly within the structure of Willow Creek Community Church. We believe this number will increase as we continue to place a central value on small groups. Many other churches throughout the world are growing in their commitment to small group ministries as well, so the need for resources is increasing.

In response to this great need, the Interactions small group series has been developed. Willow Creek Association and Zondervan have joined together to create a whole new approach to small group materials. These discussion guides are meant to challenge group members to a deeper level of sharing, create lines of accountability, move followers of Christ into action, and help group members become fully devoted followers of Christ.

SUGGESTIONS FOR INDIVIDUAL STUDY

1. Begin each session with prayer. Ask God to help you understand the passage and to apply it to your life.
2. A good modern translation, such as the New International Version, Today's New International Version, the New American Standard Bible, or the New Revised Standard Version, will give you the most help. Questions in this guide are based on the New International Version.
3. Read and reread the passage(s). You must know what the passage says before you can understand what it means and how it applies to you.
4. Write your answers in the spaces provided in the study guide. This will help you to express clearly your understanding of the passage.
5. Keep a Bible dictionary handy. Use it to look up unfamiliar words, names, or places.

SUGGESTIONS FOR GROUP STUDY

1. Come to the session prepared. Careful preparation will greatly enrich your time in group discussion.
2. Be willing to join in the discussion. The leader of the group will not be lecturing but will encourage people to discuss what they have learned in the passage. Plan to share what God has taught you in your individual study.
3. Stick to the passage being studied. Base your answers on the verses being discussed rather than on outside authorities such as commentaries or your favorite author or speaker.
4. Try to be sensitive to the other members of the group. Listen attentively when they speak, and be affirming whenever you can. This will encourage more hesitant members of the group to participate.
5. Be careful not to dominate the discussion. By all means participate, but allow others to have equal time.
6. If you are the discussion leader, you will find additional suggestions and helpful ideas in the Leader's Notes.

ADDITIONAL RESOURCES AND TEACHING MATERIALS

At the end of this study guide you will find a collection of resources and teaching materials to help you in your growth as a follower of Christ. You will also find resources that will help your church develop and build fully devoted followers of Christ.

Introduction: Clear Answers to Confusing Issues

"Mrs. Jones, I like Sunday school, and most of what we talk about makes sense. But sometimes I wonder about things like, 'Is God really out there and does He hear my prayers?'"

"Daniel, we don't question God. We just have faith and believe what the Bible says. It is not right to ask those kinds of questions!"

"Daddy, why did God let our puppy get hit by a car and then die?"

"Honey, it's not our place to ask. You just have to trust that God knows what is best."

"Pastor, sometimes I look at this world and get discouraged. Wars and conflicts seem to increase with each generation instead of decrease. We keep abusing the environment and I wonder how God feels about that. I don't know how all this stuff works, but I wonder if God has answers for all the questions swirling around in my mind."

"God is on the throne. No need to worry! Just trust and don't spend your time stewing over questions we could never answer."

Many people have asked spiritual questions and been shut down, led to think that questioning is wrong. Some people see questions as a sign of a weak faith. They discourage the practice of asking questions and don't create an atmosphere where wondering is invited.

This was not the way of Jesus.

Jesus was a rabbi, and rabbis were famous for answering a question with another question. This led to deep and meaningful theological conversations. When Jesus interacted with Nicodemus (John 3), the conversation was propelled forward by a series of questions from both men. The next chapter, John 4, records another of Jesus' interactions, this time with a woman by a well. This conversation was also peppered with questions.

What a beautiful picture! A wealthy, powerful, educated, Jewish male spiritual leader. A poor, powerless, broken Samaritan woman. In both cases they felt free to ask Jesus the questions that were on their hearts and Jesus engaged with them in rich conversation. There is no sense that He was offended by their questions ... He invited and encouraged them.

Jesus still loves to hear our questions. Those who ponder, wonder about, or even question things do not bother God. He is ready to help us grapple with our concerns and wants us to discover that there are answers. And when we can't find neat and tidy answers, He wants us to know that it is still healthy to dialogue.

In this small group study we will look at six big questions many people are asking today. God is ready to give us the wisdom and insight needed to navigate the questions that seem too big for us:

- How do we find peace in a war-torn world?
- Can our planet survive?
- How do I balance life's demands?
- Is God really out there?
- Does God hear my prayers?
- Aren't all religions the same?

Answers to these questions are not simple or simplistic. Only God has the vantage point needed to help us. He has a perspective like none other. As your group walks through these questions, talks together, looks at biblical teaching, and seeks God's wisdom, you will discover that Jesus still welcomes your questions. Through the process, your faith will grow and you will draw near to the God who is ready to help you discover answers, His presence, and joy on the journey.

How Do We Find Peace in a War-Torn World?

Have you ever watched the news coverage of world conflicts and wondered why these people can't get along? Have you ever read a column in the newspaper or a headline on your web browser about another war and found yourself thinking, "Let's just lock the leaders of these nations in a room until they can work out their differences"? Remember when you were a kid and you got into a fight with a friend, and a teacher or parent would force you to stand toe-to-toe and apologize? Why can't world conflicts be settled like that? People would just shake hands, say they are sorry, give each other a hug, and go home as friends.

It is easy for us to shake our head as we see nations at war and be baffled as to why they can't find a peaceful resolution to their conflict. It all seems so clear when we sit as armchair generals. But let's be honest. Most of us have relationships with unresolved conflict. Many who claim to follow the Prince of Peace have people in their life whom they will not forgive for a past wrong. Many Christians can't find the strength and resolve to pick up the phone, call a friend or family member, and say, "I need to apologize for how I have wronged you. Could we meet to talk things through and work toward a restored and healed relationship?"

Before we condemn the leaders of nations for not being peace-makers, it might be helpful to look inward and make sure we are taking steps of peace in our own life.

A WIDE ANGLE VIEW

1 If you have a relationship that is conflicted and needs restoration, what is getting in the way of you doing your part to seek healing?

A BIBLICAL PORTRAIT

Centuries before Jesus was born, the prophet Isaiah wrote of the coming Messiah and said:

For to us a child is born,
to us a son is given,
and the government will be on his shoulders.
And he will be called
Wonderful Counselor, Mighty God,
Everlasting Father, **Prince of Peace**.
Of the increase of his government and peace
there will be no end.
He will reign on David's throne
and over his kingdom,
establishing and upholding it
with justice and righteousness
from that time on and forever.
The zeal of the LORD Almighty
will accomplish this. (Isa. 9:6 – 7, emphasis added)

When Jesus was born, the heavenly host declared:

Glory to God in the highest,
and on earth **peace** *to men on whom his favor rests. (Luke 2:14,*
emphasis added)

In the Sermon on the Mount, the most famous message ever preached, there is a section called the Beatitudes in which Jesus said:

"Blessed are the **peacemakers**,
*   for they will be called sons of God." (Matt. 5:9, emphasis added)*

Before Jesus died on the cross, He gave these words of comfort to His followers:

"All this I have spoken while still with you. But the Counselor, the Holy Spirit, whom the Father will send in my name, will teach you all things and will remind you of everything I have said to you. **Peace I leave with you; my peace I give you**. *I do not give to you as the world gives. Do not let your hearts be troubled and do not be afraid." (John 14:25–27, emphasis added)*

After Jesus had risen from the dead and ascended to heaven, Peter preached the good news saying:

I now realize how true it is that God does not show favoritism but accepts men from every nation who fear him and do what is right. You know the message God sent to the people of Israel, telling **the good news of peace through Jesus Christ**, *who is Lord of all. (Acts 10:34–36, emphasis added)*

2 How does the theme of peace weave its way through the life and teaching of Jesus?

3 If we are to reflect the heart and will of God in the world, how will this impact the way we seek peace in *one* of the following areas:

- Our personal relationships?
- Our community?
- Our churches?
- The world?

SHARPENING THE FOCUS

Read Snapshot "The Ultimate Warmonger"

THE ULTIMATE WARMONGER

"The thief comes only to steal and kill and destroy; I have come that they may have life, and have it to the full." (John 10:10)

"You belong to your father, the devil, and you want to carry out your father's desire. He was a murderer from the beginning, not holding to the truth, for there is no truth in him. When he lies, he speaks his native language, for he is a liar and the father of lies." (John 8:44)

Be self-controlled and alert. Your enemy the devil prowls around like a roaring lion looking for someone to devour. (1 Peter 5:8)

Jesus came to bring peace. Satan, on the other hand, loves to bring war, conflict, tension, dissension, and division. His strategy in this world is to sow seeds of strife between brothers, sisters, business partners, politicians, and world leaders. Satan knows that a little strife, mixed with the depraved nature of men and women, can create the perfect storm of hatred, malice, and war. If we look back over the last couple of centuries, it looks like the enemy's tactics are working fairly well. War and collateral damage are everywhere . . . in homes, churches, communities, and between nations.

4 Looking around the world today, what are some signs that Satan's tactics are still working to create conflict, dissension, and war in the following areas:

- Our marriages?

- Our families?

- Our churches?

- Our communities and nations?

Read Snapshot "Deal with It"

DEAL WITH IT

"If your brother sins against you, go and show him his fault, just between the two of you. If he listens to you, you have won your brother over." (Matt. 18:15)

When conflict exists in one of our relationships, who should try to resolve it? We should! It doesn't matter who started it.

Jesus' teaching on dealing with relational conflict is simple and clear: You go. Go in private. Don't send a bunch of emails about how so-and-so did a bunch of nasty stuff to you. Don't go with an accusing spirit. Go to seek a restored relationship, not to pick a bigger fight. The passage goes on to give additional steps to take if this approach does not bring about a restored relationship, but this is the first step for all of us.

5

Of course, we can refuse to follow Jesus' approach to conflict resolution. What are some of the consequences if we ignore His direction and decide to:

- Stuff down our hurt and refuse to talk with the person?

- Tell others about how we have been hurt by this person?

- Come with an accusatory spirit?

- Be defensive and view everything as an attack?

6

What Jesus says makes perfect sense, but it is so hard to do. What gets in the way of seeking a reconciled relationship when someone has wronged you?

Without using a name or specific situation, how can your group members pray for you and keep you accountable to seek reconciliation in a broken relationship you may be dealing with?

Read Snapshot "Walk Out of a Worship Service"

WALK OUT OF A WORSHIP SERVICE

"Therefore, if you are offering your gift at the altar and there remember that your brother has something against you, leave your gift there in front of the altar. First go and be reconciled to your brother; then come and offer your gift." (Matt. 5:23–24)

There is only one reason the Bible gives to get up and walk out of a worship service. It is found in this passage. When we are trying to worship God and we remember that we are living with unresolved conflict with a brother or sister, we have permission to get up and go make things right in the relationship. It might mean saying, "I was wrong, will you forgive me?" It could mean setting up a time to meet and have a good old-fashioned truth-telling session. But peace in our relationships is so important that God actually encourages us to go get things right before we turn our attention to worshiping Him.

I have preached on this passage and topic many times over the years. I remember one time when the anointing of the Holy Spirit was clear and powerful. During the message people began to get up and walk out of the worship center. This was before cell phones so they lined up five- and six-deep at the pay phones in the church lobby, calling people to say: "We need to meet," "I want to tell you I'm sorry," "I would really like to reconcile." I believe heaven celebrated as walls were torn down, healing came, and interpersonal wars ceased.

7

What is the relationship between being a healthy worshiper of Jesus and living with healed and reconciled relationships?

Read Snapshot "Commit to Peace"

COMMIT TO PEACE

If it is possible, as far as it depends on you, live at peace with everyone. (Rom. 12:18)

Not everyone in this life will like us. Sorry to be the bearer of bad news, but this is just part of life's journey. Some people are conflict-oriented, like to pick fights, and don't play well with others. This does not give us license to be nasty in return. As a matter of fact, Jesus is clear that we need to do our part to make peace and reflect His love for relational harmony.

If we feel a relationship is conflicted, we need to seek peace (even if we are not the instigator of the conflict). Then, once we have done all we can, we might have to live with the fact that another person refuses restoration. If we have done our part, we can have inner peace even when a relationship remains conflicted. And we can leave the door open, praying that one day the other person may be ready to walk through it and seek healing in the relationship.

8

Most of us have been in a relationship where we have tried to seek peace but the other person refused. When this happens, what have you done to:

- Seek inner peace about this conflicted relationship that you have tried to restore?

- Keep the door open to this person so they know you are ready to seek peace as soon as they are willing to take a step forward?

Read Snapshot "Will Wars Ever Cease?"

WILL WARS EVER CEASE?

"You will hear of wars and rumors of wars, but see to it that you are not alarmed. Such things must happen, but the end is still to come." (Matt. 24:6)

Jesus is clear that wars and rumors of wars will continue until the end of time. Yes, we are called to be peacemakers ... all the days of our lives. No, wars will never be gone completely. The sinful nature of human beings guarantees that conflicts, wars, and brokenness in human community will be part of life's landscape until Jesus comes again and makes all things right.

The reality that wars and human conflict will be part of life should not cause us to throw up our hands and quit seeking peace. It should do exactly the opposite. The reality that war and relational conflict will always be with us should cause us to walk even closer with the Prince of Peace and seek to be His agents of peace wherever we go.

9 What is one specific place and practical way you can be a peacemaker right where God has placed you? How can your group members pray for you and encourage you in your efforts to bring the peace of Jesus to this situation?

PUTTING YOURSELF IN THE PICTURE

MAKE A CALL

We all deal with conflict in relationships. Who is one person in your life right now who feels estranged from you because of conflict in the relationship?

Call them. Pray first, asking God for a humble heart. But just make the call. Apologize for where you have been wrong. Tell them that you want a restored relationship and inquire what you can do to make things right. If this person is a follower of Jesus, ask if you can pray together before the conversation is over.

OPEN THE DOOR

If you have tried to reconcile with someone but they have refused, do this one simple thing ... leave the door open. Call them, email them, text them, or write a note to say that you are there for them whenever they are ready to talk and begin the healing process.

CAN OUR PLANET SURVIVE?

REFLECTIONS FROM SESSION 1

1. How have you noticed Satan trying to create conflict and division in your relationships, workplace, neighborhood, church, or elsewhere? What have you been doing to battle his warmongering ways?

2. If you went to someone and tried to live out Jesus' teaching from Matthew 18:15, how did it go? How did you feel taking this action, and how did the other person respond?

THE BIG PICTURE

Christians know that Genesis teaches about how God made the heavens and the earth and, as Creator, cares about all He has made. But the theme of God's concern for creation is not limited to the first book of the Bible—it's found throughout the entire Scriptures.

Did you know that God is concerned about *Soil-Abuse*? In Leviticus 26:33–35, God rebuked His people for not resting the land that they were farming. Land, by His decree, should lie fallow—be rested and refurbished—before being farmed again. God knew that such a Sabbathlike planting rhythm was a healthy thing, yet the people refused to obey this wisdom.

God also banned *Tree-Abuse*. Often, in ancient times, an attacking army would destroy all of the trees in a city because they did not want the people of the land using the fruit to sustain themselves and eventually become a military threat again in the future. But God prohibited such activity: "When you lay siege to a city for a long time, fighting against it to capture it, do not destroy its trees by putting an ax to them, because you can eat their fruit. Do not cut them down. Are the trees of the field people, that you should besiege them?" (Deut. 20:19) In essence, He was saying, "You might be in a battle with the people of a city, but the trees are not at fault ... leave them alone."

A third example of God's concern for His creation is His warning against what could be called *Animal-Abuse*. In Proverbs 12:10 we read, "A righteous man cares for the needs of his animal." There is a clear sense that God cares for the creatures He has made and He expects us to care for them as well.

God says, "Everything in creation is mine. Treat it respectfully. Subdue it, rule over it, work it, but protect it and take care of it. No abuse allowed."

A WIDE ANGLE VIEW

1

What is one way you see our society abusing and hurting God's creation?

What is one way you have not cared for creation as you could and should have?

A BIBLICAL PORTRAIT

Read Genesis 1 and Psalm 24:1–2

2

A piece of art tells something about the artist. What do you learn about God by looking at His creation (from mountains and deserts to oceans, from the smallest microscopic particles to the vastness of galaxies to the complexity of human beings)?

3

How does God view His creation, and how should this impact how we see it?

How should this influence how we treat creation?

SHARPENING THE FOCUS

Read Snapshot "Subdue, Rule, Work, and Care"

SUBDUE, RULE, WORK, AND CARE

*God blessed them and said to them, "Be fruitful and increase in number; fill the earth and **subdue** it. **Rule** over the fish of the sea and the birds of the air and over every living creature that moves on the ground." (Gen. 1:28, emphasis added)*

*The LORD God took the man and put him in the Garden of Eden to **work** it and take **care** of it. (Gen. 2:15, emphasis added)*

The oceans, forests, plains, rivers, lakes — all creation belongs to God. The old hymn puts it this way, *This Is My Father's World*. In the early chapters of Genesis, God gives four key instructions on planet care:

Subdue. This does not mean to misuse, abuse, or beat into submission. The word connotes bringing something into conformity when it gets unruly. It is *not* right to chop down trees when attacking a city, but it *is* appropriate to trim back a tree growing across a path or that might crash down on your house.

Rule. This word connotes having authority. In fact, it's the same word used for how a parent relates to a child. It's about bringing things to a sense of orderliness and developing positive traits over time. People are given authority over the earth, but are not to misuse that authority.

Work. If you have ever farmed or even had a garden, you know it takes work to yield a crop. It means tilling, planting, weeding, watering, and perhaps other regular activities. Do this and the land will become fruitful. If we want the earth to remain healthy and fruitful, we will have to do our part. It takes work.

Care. The word used here carries the idea of protecting something and keeping it safe. This instruction helps us see that we are to do more than just refrain from abusing the earth. We have a sacred duty to protect the glorious creation God has made. We are to care for the earth.

---

4 Some people have taken the ideas of subduing and ruling the earth as license to do whatever we want with God's creation. How does this errant interpretation cause problems:

- In how we treat the earth?

- In how some Christians are viewed by a world that has increasing concern for the planet?

5 The Scriptures declare that God cares about all of His creation. What can we do to partner with Him in taking care of the earth?

Read Snapshot "Creation Gives Witness to God"

CREATION GIVES WITNESS TO GOD

... since what may be known about God is plain to them, because God has made it plain to them. For since the creation of the world God's invisible qualities — his eternal power and divine nature — have been clearly seen, being understood from what has been made, so that men are without excuse. (Rom. 1:19–20)

> *The heavens declare the glory of God;*
> *the skies proclaim the work of his hands.*
> *Day after day they pour forth speech;*
> *night after night they display knowledge.*
> *There is no speech or language*
> *where their voice is not heard.*
> *Their voice goes out into all the earth,*
> *their words to the ends of the world. (Ps. 19:1–4)*

The power, beauty, design, and glory of God's creation is an affirmation of His presence to both believers and seekers. Any logical, honest person who beholds the creative realm has to conclude that an Intelligent Designer is behind it all, and Scripture teaches us that people have to lie to themselves and others if they are going to insist otherwise. Creation itself is an apologetic for the existence of God. It is a powerful witness.

6

Tell about one place in creation that really speaks to you about the presence and power of God.

How does God speak to you when you meet with Him in this place?

Read Snapshot "Creation Gives Us Places to Connect with God"

CREATION GIVES US PLACES TO CONNECT WITH GOD

God knows that His people need to be in the context of His created splendor in order to become quiet before Him. In mountain pastures or on desert sands, on or beside a lake or ocean, under a shade tree at a local park, we can find a tranquil place to experience deep spiritual reflection and hear God's voice with greater clarity.

Jesus understood this. If you study the Gospels, you discover that He spent much of His time around and on the Sea of Galilee. Jesus also had a habit of going off by Himself into quiet places in the hills, wilderness, and desert. In these places He met with the Father and found spiritual refreshment. What an example for us. If Jesus sought quiet times and places in creation, how much more should we?

7

Why do you think Jesus spent so much of His discretionary time by the Sea of Galilee and other places that brought Him close to nature?

What can you learn from His example?

Read Snapshot "The Bad News and the Good News"

THE BAD NEWS AND THE GOOD NEWS

 God created the earth. He called us to work it and care for it. He reveals His artistic beauty and amazing design in creation. And the wonder of nature can connect us closely with its Artist. This is all good news. But there is bad news. As a human family we have been careless and have abused the world God made and declared, "Very good!"

Due to our mismanagement of creation, about a third of the earth's soil is now unfit for growing food because of the overuse of fertilizers and poor waste disposal practices. There are about twenty major cities around the world with air pollution indexes so high that government officials encourage citizens to wear breathing masks to and from work. Rainforests that once covered 14 percent of the earth and are key to the entire global ecosystem have been reduced to about 6 percent. Oceans, rivers, lakes, and streams are becoming increasingly polluted, which compromises the drinking water of up to a billion people in underdeveloped parts of the world. These abuses affect all of us but they have a greater impact on the poor in developing countries, which means they suffer disproportionately when the environment is abused. That's the bad news . . . and every follower of Jesus should take it seriously.

The good news is that there is a growing awareness and concern among Christians. We are rising up, expressing concern, and taking action. Many corporations, communities, and countries are also beginning to take action. Cars that use to spew out pollution are now running much cleaner. Areas where people use to burn leaves and trash now have better sanitation. Cities that once sat under a layer of smog now have cleaner air. Many rivers and ponds once poisoned with factory waste are now running clean. This is all good news, and we should celebrate it.

8

When it comes to caring for creation, what is a good sign you have seen in our society, the church, or your own life?

What can we do to increase a positive concern for the creation?

9

Where do you believe Christians and the church need to take another step forward in caring for God's creation?

What can the members of your small group do to engage in this action?

PUTTING YOURSELF IN THE PICTURE

DOING OUR PART

Sometimes little things make a big difference. Review the information below, and then identify one or two ways you can start to do your part for creation care:

New Light Bulbs. Compact fluorescent bulbs use 75 percent less electricity than regular bulbs. If every home in the U.S. replaced just one light bulb with a compact fluorescent, we'd save enough energy to light more than 2.5 million homes per year. The compact fluorescent bulbs cost about twice as much but they last much longer and burn much less energy.

Bottled Water. In 2008, Americans threw away about thirty-eight billion plastic water bottles that were buried in landfills. If we simply used filtered water and refilled bottles, we would impact the environment in great ways.

Water-Saving Faucets. If a family of four put in water-saving faucets they could save up to 20,000 gallons of water a year.

Room Temperature. If you turned your thermostat down by an average of three degrees you could save up to 10 percent of your energy usage.

CONNECT WITH GOD

Make time in the coming week to find a quiet place in creation. This might mean taking a long walk outdoors or just sitting in a park. Look around. Drink in the beauty. Notice God's handiwork. Thank God for the wonder of all He has made. Then, in this quiet place, read Genesis 1 and Psalm 24:1–2 and pray for a heart that cares about creation the way God does. Commit to do your part to care for the one and only planet we have.

How Do I Balance Life's Demands?

Reflections from Session 2

1. If you have started looking at the earth, ecology, and the use of resources in new ways, share this with your group.
2. If you have taken a step to help impact the world in a positive way (light bulbs, water bottles, room temperature, recycling ... anything), tell about what you have done and how this new action makes you feel.

THE BIG PICTURE

How do most people respond these days when casually asked, "How are you doing?" More and more I hear them answer, "Hangin' in there," "I am so busy," "I'm stretched thin," "I'm burning the candle at both ends," "I just feel burned out," "I can't remember the last time I took a day off," or "Life is just a blur!" In some cases these declarations are made with a sense of resigned desperation; in others, with a sense of subtle pride and bragging. But every time I hear people talk like this I wonder, what will it take for us to live with balance and health in a world with growing demands?

It seems that people complain about the crowdedness and hurriedness of their lives more than ever. This is ironic because we've been sold a wheelbarrow full of time-saving, life-simplifying devices over the last couple decades—everything from computers to PDAs to cell phones to microwaves to super-fast vegetable choppers. Sadly, almost every current study shows that the average American worker is putting in longer hours, commuting longer distances, carting more work home, and taking fewer days off as well as shorter vacations. What's more, most of us are spending less time with our spouse and children, less time pursuing recreation, and less time in church.

If we are not careful, the pace of life will keep accelerating to the point that we will race past all the things that matter most. For some of us this has already become a painful reality. In light of the ever-increasing complexity and pace of life, we should all ask ourselves this important question: *What experience of enduring value can occur at a very, very high rate of speed?*

Can you experience and sustain deep levels of marital intimacy with your foot on the accelerator of life? Does this pace lend itself to sensitive, self-disclosing, intimacy-enhancing conversations with your spouse? Can you really know what's going on in the heart of a ten-year-old child when you are moving at full speed? Does a parent connect deeply with their kids while sprinting through each day? Can you invest in deep, rich friendships if you never block out time for your friends? Can you figure out the guiding hand of God or hear His voice with clarity while living in the fast lane?

The truth is that the most treasured times with family, friends, and God are done slowly. Intimacy can't be microwaved. A quietness surrounds the things in life that matter most. They are experienced in moments when the time frame is open-ended.

A WIDE ANGLE VIEW

1 Respond to *one* of the following questions:

- What one "time-saving device" didn't really save you any time?
- Do you find yourself more or less busy now than you were five years ago, and why?
- What pace of life has created the most open space for rich relational connections and spiritual growth?

A BIBLICAL PORTRAIT

Read Ecclesiastes 3:1–8 and Isaiah 30:15–16

2 Ecclesiastes teaches that there is enough time for everything in life. What is one thing mentioned in this passage that you would like to make more time for, and how can you make space for it?

The Isaiah passage depicts a dramatic contrast between the pace of life God wants for His children and how fast we actually live. How do you see this same contrast alive in our lives today?

SHARPENING THE FOCUS

Read Snapshot "Speed Versus Soul"

SPEED VERSUS SOUL

The faster we move, the more our soul dwindles. The more cluttered our outward life, the harder it is to nurture our inner life of faith. With this in mind, it is important to identify the things that tend to amp us to the breaking point, three culprits being:

Increased Opportunities. The sheer volume of exciting, entertaining, and developmental opportunities available to people today is staggering. When I was a kid there weren't twenty-seven professional sports leagues available at all times. We had one black-and-white TV set with poor reception on two channels. There were no video games or Internet (there were actually no home PCs). My family sat down for dinner together every evening. Life was much simpler. Today the smorgasbord of opportunities for kids and adults is so big it is easy to speed up as we try to do everything.

Competitiveness. The world is becoming more and more competitive. For kids it starts early; from school to sports, they are driven to win. For adults who work in the marketplace they are facing the reality that most companies have higher goals, lower expenses, and thinner margins. To survive, companies must be more competitive — and this means longer work days, bigger workloads, a faster pace, and sometimes even lower pay. This cultural competitiveness speeds up our pace of life and limits time for soul development.

Stimulation Overload. It doesn't require extensive research (although there is!) to realize that high-power and high-tech input is filling our lives in ever-increasing measure. In one weekend a person can go to a rock concert with a mind-splitting light and sound show, watch a movie in a Cineplex with twenty options, get into a car with a stereo so powerful it could explode their ear drums, get on a plane and travel cross-country while working on a computer, and "relax" by playing a video game on a hand-held device. The list of technical options could go on and on.

With the increased opportunities, growing competitiveness, and proliferation of technical stimulation, it's not hard to see why life is speeding up and soul-space is dwindling.

3

How have you seen one of these three factors impact the pace of your life?

How can we combat these things that are increasing our pace?

Read Snapshot "Just Say No"

JUST SAY NO

One of the best ways to dial back our frenzied pace of life is to learn one simple, single-syllable word. No!

If we are going to make space to grow our soul and strike a healthy balance in our life, we will have to boldly decline many of the wonderful opportunities life affords. The fact is . . . we can't do it all. If we try to, it will kill us!

The key is to have the wisdom to know what matters most and to avoid the things that are not as important. Along with wisdom we must have courage. When we say no, we can be sure that some people won't understand and others won't like it. We might just incur the displeasure of people . . . maybe even people we care about. But we are responsible to set a pace of life that creates balance and keeps our soul healthy.

---

4 Tell about a time you set boundaries and said no. What resulted from your decision to draw this line and seek to live with balance?

5 In what area of your life have you overextended yourself and need to set boundaries and say no?

How can your group members pray for you and keep you accountable to follow through on setting boundaries in this area of your life?

Read Snapshot "You Win"

YOU WIN

 In my younger days I thought I needed to compete and win in every single arena of life. Many of us live with this kind of attitude. Over time God has taught me that I don't need to be competitive all the time. There is nothing wrong with healthy competition, but there are times to simply dial back and not worry about ending up on top. There are times to look at others and say, "You win!" There are also situations when it is best to not even enter into the competitive fray.

For one person this could mean saying, "I don't have to get the top grade in every one of my classes." To another it might mean declaring, "This year I will not spend countless hours setting up a Christmas light display at my house." For yet another it might mean saying, "You can go after the promotion. I don't need to battle to climb the next rung of the ladder." Such statements are not a sign of apathy or resignation. They can actually be a declaration that something else matters more than winning. When we let go of a pathological obsession with competition we can embrace freedom and breathe in the liberation of contentment.

---

6 How have you seen the increasing drive to compete and win impact the lives of children, teens, and adults in our culture?

7 In what area of your life might competition and winning be too important?

How might your life simplify and become more balanced if you were a little more content and a little less competitive in this area of life?

Read Snapshot "Sensory Control"

SENSORY CONTROL

Another way to strike balance in our life is to intentionally limit our exposure to experiences that bring sensory overload. Some things tend to fry our nerve endings and titillate our senses. But louder, bigger, and more does not always mean better. We find balance in our lives and nurture for our souls when we rediscover the simple pleasures of life that are unplugged and natural.

The stuff that makes life worth living happens across a table with a fellow traveler in life. Balance comes as we take a walk with a spouse, child, or friend and have a simple conversation. Sitting for an hour in a chair on the porch or in the yard can be one of the most valuable things we could do. Speed and soul are inextricably bound up in an inverse relationship. The higher our speed, the less healthy our soul; the more we discover quiet and simplicity, the stronger our soul can grow. This is not a diatribe against technology or exciting experiences. But it *is* an appeal for balance. Along with big sensory experiences should come times of silence and reflection.

8

Use the scale below to indicate how you tend to live your life:

I tend toward quiet
times of reflection
and silence

I live with a healthy balance
of sensory-stimulation and
times of quiet

I naturally like
high levels of
sensory-stimulation

| 1 | 2 | 3 | 4 | 5 | 6 | 7 | 8 | 9 | 10 |

9

What is one source of sensory input that you could turn off (or tune down) for the next month, and how might you invest this time into a specific relationship that needs to be strengthened and nurtured?

PUTTING YOURSELF IN THE PICTURE

THREE SOUL QUESTIONS

Through the years I have used three questions to help me determine how I am doing in growing my soul. Take time to ask each of these questions in the coming week and evaluate how you are doing:

Soul Question 1: *Do I feel alive and buoyant in my inner person these days?*

When this is the case we can sense the springs of God's living water welling up in us. We feel fresh and full on the inside. If we are not paying appropriate attention to our soul, we begin to describe our inner condition as "barren, empty, dry, or arid."

Soul Question 2: *Is my soul more responsive to the activity of God throughout the day?*

When our soul is expanding and fresh, we grow increasingly aware of God's closeness and work. We feel His promptings, sense His nudging, see His smile, and know His affirmation. Then, when we know God is leading and directing, we are ready to follow Him.

Soul Question 3: *Is my soul more or less responsive to the souls of other people?*

The Bible teaches that when our soul is well cared for, growing, and nurtured, it will seek out soulful conversations with fellow travelers. We won't want to just talk on a superficial level. We will want to share life with other people on the level where we feel alive ... on a soul level.

SPEED CONTROL

It's speed versus soul.

If you don't care if your soul becomes dry and unresponsive to God, then keep your foot on the accelerator and speed through life. If speed means more to you than soul, then enjoy the ride — but realize that you are giving up something very important! If, on the other hand, you want to grow your soul, make space for God, and go deep with people, you will need to learn how to control your speed.

It was Carl Jung who said, "Hurry is not of the devil; it is the devil!" Look over your schedule from the past month. Where were you busy and hurried, and where did you have space for rest and a slower pace? Now look ahead at the coming month. Make space for quiet, Sabbath, play, unscheduled time with the people you love, and generous space to sit quietly at the feet of Jesus. The only person who can control the speed of your life is you. Make decisions that will enhance your soul.

IS GOD REALLY OUT THERE?

REFLECTIONS FROM SESSION 3

1. If you have been trying to reduce your speed so you can grow your soul, how is this going? If you are finding some quiet places, how is this helping you connect more closely with God?

2. If you have gone out on a limb and said no for the sake of living a more balanced life, describe this experience. How did you feel and how did the recipient of your no handle it?

THE BIG PICTURE

Throughout the course of life we will have friends and acquaintances who doubt the reality and existence of God. Some will freely admit that they have never really invested much intellectual energy in trying to resolve their doubts. They think, "If there is a God, He's going to do His thing and I'm going to do mine. It will all turn out in the end."

We will also connect with people who roll up their sleeves and do the rigorous work of reading, studying, questioning, and reflecting on God's existence. Many of these people will eventually come to a firm conviction that there is a God and He wants to be a part of their life.

As followers of Jesus, we need to be ready to help people move forward on this journey of faith. When we meet people who are struggling with the question, "Is God really out there?" we can help them see how God is alive and at work in the world. One of the most natural ways to do this is by helping them notice the splendor and intricacy of creation.

Imagine that one fine mid-spring morning you are having a cup of coffee with a friend who is not sure God exists. All of a sudden you see a blur of color outside your kitchen window. You both say, at almost the same time, "Look, a hummingbird!" This moment could easily become a conversation starter about the wonder and beauty of creation. Hummingbirds can fly forward, backward, sideways, even upside down. They flap their wings about a hundred times per second; their heart can beat over 1,200 times per minute. These simple facts might just open the door to talk about the artistic God who made it.

A WIDE ANGLE VIEW

1

What is one place in creation where you consistently experience the beauty and power of God? Why do you feel this place connects you with God in such deep ways?

A BIBLICAL PORTRAIT

Read Psalm 19:1–6; Psalm 8:1–9; Romans 1:20; and Genesis 1:1–5

2

What do these passages teach us about the relationship of God to the heavens, earth, and all of creation?

3

What are some ways God reveals Himself to human beings through the staggering beauty and intricate design of creation?

SHARPENING THE FOCUS

Read Snapshot "Intelligent Design"

INTELLIGENT DESIGN

Sometimes when I talk to someone about the existence of God I begin by talking about the human eye. I'll say, "Did you know that on a clear day the human eye can easily see an elevated object forty miles away?" I tell them that when I take a boat across Lake Michigan, on a clear day I can easily see the top of Chicago's Sears Tower more than forty miles from shore. Then, within a fraction of a second, that same eye can refocus on a single grain of salt on my fingertip. I'll ask, "How many shades of color do you think the human eye can differentiate?" They usually guess, "About a hundred?" They are always surprised when I tell them it is actually over a thousand. I also inform them that the human eye is made up of a hundred million individual light cells that all work together in a coordinated fashion to provide human beings with this remarkable thing called vision. Finally I'll ask, "Is something so sophisticated and well coordinated more likely the result of intelligent design or the consequence of a cosmic accidental collision of gases a few billion years ago?"

I encourage people who have serious doubts about God's existence to take walks in creation, to spend an afternoon at the zoo, to go scuba diving for a day, to watch the sun set in the Western sky. I invite them to honestly reflect and calculate the odds of all of those wonders being caused by an accidental explosion somewhere in the forgotten past. Or might there just be a loving and creative God who fashioned and created all we see?

4 Tell about a time God clearly revealed Himself to you as you experienced His presence and power unveiled in creation.

Imagine you are talking with a spiritual seeker about a hummingbird, the human eye, or a place of amazing beauty in creation. What might you say that could open the way for a spiritual conversation?

Read Snapshot "Moral Oughtness"

MORAL OUGHTNESS

Every human being lives with a sense of what could be called "moral oughtness." This is the gut sense that some things simply ought not to happen. Some things are just . . . wrong. And, conversely, other things ought to happen because they are clearly right.

Sometimes when I meet a person who is not sure God is really out there, I engage in a conversation about the moral center that seems to exist in all people everywhere. For instance, when we hear about another school shooting, an "investor" walking away with millions of dollars as elderly people lose their life savings, or parents abusing their child, something inside of us cries out, "Injustice!" Hundreds of millions of diverse people all agree that these are immoral acts.

Cultures around the world agree that truth-telling is preferred to lying, that kindness should trump violence, that loyalty is better than betrayal, that justice should win over injustice. It almost appears that a supreme moral being deposited something in the soul of human beings that results in this inner moral code, this sense of "oughtness."

5
Name some things that virtually everyone in the world believes are wrong.

Now name some things that are commended and affirmed by people worldwide.

6
How does this sense of "moral oughtness" in the hearts and minds of human beings point to the existence of a God?

What would the world be like if we affirmed that human beings are simply evolved organisms with no need to follow moral codes or our inner sense of right and wrong?

Read Snapshot "Personal Testimony"

PERSONAL TESTIMONY

 As we encounter people who wonder if God is really out there, we can look with amazement at the intelligent design of the universe and ponder the existence of a heavenly designer. We also can reflect on the existence of a moral center that exists in all people. And we can simply tell our story of how we have encountered God. Each man, woman, and child who has a relationship with God through faith in Jesus Christ has a story to tell.

Telling our story is not about memorizing a specific script that we regurgitate every time we meet a spiritual seeker. Instead, it is a natural and organic expression of things such as:

- How we first came to a place of putting our faith in God
- Who Jesus is to us and how He is working in our life
- How our life has changed since we entered a saving relationship with Jesus
- How God has been at work in our life recently

This testimony takes many shapes and forms because God is always doing new things in our life.

7

Share a testimony with your group members. Using one of the bullet points above, express an element of who God is to you and how Jesus is working in your life.

Read Snapshot "Planting a Seed ... Do Versus Done"

PLANTING A SEED ... DO VERSUS DONE

 While on a sailing vacation together, Lynne and I pulled into a harbor, dropped anchor, and went ashore. As we walked along a crescent, white-sand beach, a guy stopped us and said, "Did you just drop anchor in that boat out there?" When I said yes, he enthusiastically responded, "Well, we're on the boat next to you and wondered if you'd like to come over for happy hour later this afternoon." I was thinking, "I wonder how happy this crowd gets?" but Lynne and I decided to go.

As we visited with the group of couples on the deck of their boat, the sun was going down and so were rum punches, pina coladas, and lots of drinks I had never heard of. At one point in the evening's conversation a woman says, "So, Bill, what do you do for a living?" I just put it right out there and said, "Well, I'm a minister." And they said, "Ooooh, we got ourselves a minister! Pour another one!" It actually led to a fun conversation. Sometime later, just as Lynne and I were getting ready to head out, one of our new friends said, "Hey, Bill! I always wanted to ask a sincere Christian how they ended up that way. Could you take a minute and tell us how you became a Christian?"

There stood a dozen people, drinks in hands, eyes fixed on me, and genuine interest in their eyes. I knew I did not have time for a thirty-minute gospel presentation, but I wanted to plant a seed. So I used a simple little illustration that has helped me plant seeds in many hearts through the years.

I simply said, "In the first part of my life I thought Christianity was spelled D-O. I thought it was about those things I do to try to climb my way up to God. Do I go to church? Do I follow the rules? Do I give money? Then I learned from the Bible that Christianity would be better spelled D-O-N-E. It's all about what God has done. God loved me. Jesus died on the cross to take away all my sins. He rose from the dead. Jesus offers forgiveness. God has reached out to me and offers His love." I went on to say, "When I discovered all God has done for me I embraced it and put my faith and trust in Jesus. I've followed Him ever since, and it has made all the difference in the world." I offered, "I'm on that boat over there and if any of you want to talk about this more, please feel free to drop by."

---

8 Some people see faith as being all about what we do. What are some things we try to do to gain God's favor, and why do these actions always fall short?

If we believe Christianity is really about what we do, how might this impact the way we live our faith?

9

The Christian faith is based on what God has DONE
for us. What are some things God has done for you,
and how could you tell others about His goodness in
your life?

PUTTING YOURSELF IN THE PICTURE

PRACTICE TELLING YOUR STORY

Take time before your next group gathering to practice telling
your testimony. Find a Christian you respect and trust and
share some of your story with them. Use the four bullet points
in the "Personal Testimony" Snapshot (page 39) as you prepare. Seek to be natural, to use common language, and to capture the truth of how God is alive and at work in your life. Ask
this person to give you input and help you express your testimony in a way that is clear and concise.

LOOK FOR GOD'S AMAZING DESIGN

Take a walk and use the time to look closely at what God has
created. Make a point of slowing down and noticing ways
God has revealed His character and intricate design in creation. As you notice God's fingerprints all over creation, pray
for opportunities to talk about these things with a friend who
is unsure if God exists.

Does God Hear My Prayers?

1. Since you have been sensitized to the wonder of God's creation, how have you noticed His intelligent design since your last group gathering?
2. If you had an opportunity to share your personal testimony or to plant a few seeds of the gospel since your last meeting, tell about this experience. How did the other person respond?

THE BIG PICTURE

Christians pray. But not all prayer is true prayer nor does everything that floats heavenward under the name of "prayer" really hit the bull's-eye. Indeed, some things that pass for prayer should be done away with or at least evaluated and revised so that they actually reach the heart of God.

Here are some types of prayer that I think we should spend some time evaluating:

Autopilot Prayers. These are prayers we can sail through or click off without even thinking. It could be a meal prayer, a bedtime prayer, even a recitation of the Lord's Prayer. It could be a prayer we memorized as a child. When we do an autopilot prayer, we say the words but our heart is not engaged with the heart of God. If the truth were known, we are just going through the motions.

Token Prayers. These are prayers that we toss out because it is the right thing to do. Before a meal we want to get to the food, but we have to pray. So we rattle off a quick, "God is great, God is good, let us thank Him for our food. Amen." Or we say a quick prayer at the start of a church meeting because that's how we're supposed to start a church meeting. It may be perfunctory, but we make sure we do it. We don't really cry out for the Spirit of God to lead and give wisdom, we just give a token, "Bless this meeting," and get to our business.

Official Prayers. Formal community settings, some school gatherings, and even governmental meetings often include an official prayer or invocation. These are often watered-down, generic prayers that have to fit all faith expressions and not offend anyone. Sometimes a list of rules (do's and don'ts) is given to the person who is asked to offer this kind of prayer (for instance, they may say God but shouldn't mention Jesus).

Preaching Prayers. This is a prayer that ends up being a sermon or message for the others who are gathered. In no real sense is the prayer being lifted to God; it is a platform to tell the others what they need to hear. It can be a parent praying with their kids, but really explaining how the kids' behavior should change. It can be a spouse explaining how the other spouse ought to behave differently. It could even be a board member who wants to let the pastor know about a concern but they frame their message as a prayer.

Preparation Prayers. As a pastor I have had people ask to pray before we begin a conversation. If they pray, "Dear Lord, please help Bill understand that I love him, and prepare his heart for what I am going to share," I know that I am about to be blasted. In these situations prayer becomes a buffer to prepare us for the bad news.

Impression Prayers. This is when someone uses prayer to let us know how spiritual they are, or to name-drop, or to inform us about how great their life is. If we are not careful, prayer can spiral down into an opportunity for us to impress others.

These are just some of the ways prayer can get off-track. If we want to grow in our communication with God, it is helpful to honestly identify where our prayer life has become far less than what it could and should be.

A WIDE ANGLE VIEW

1 How have you observed one of these prayers, and how do you think God feels when His children pray this way?

What is one kind of pseudo-prayer that you can be tempted to fall into, and what might you do to avoid this temptation?

A BIBLICAL PORTRAIT

Read Luke 18:9–14

2 What do you learn about each man in this parable simply by watching them and listening to their prayer?

SHARPENING THE FOCUS

Read Snapshot "Prayer Reveals How You See God"

PRAYER REVEALS HOW YOU SEE GOD

The Pharisee. As the Pharisee prayed, he revealed a number of things about his understanding of God. First, it seems he drastically underestimated God's ability to see matters of the heart. He really didn't think that God looks beyond the externals. Second, he underestimated God's holiness. This Pharisee piously thought he was very close to God's standard — perhaps just a step below. Third, he thoroughly misunderstood what God values. God is not drawn to self-righteousness, but to contrition and humility. Finally, he totally misunderstood justification. He thought he would be accepted in God's sight by listing all of his spiritual achievements. He believed justification is attained by works and not by grace.

The Tax Collector. This man lifted up a simple prayer, just one line: "God, have mercy on me, a sinner." First, his prayer showed that he knew God sees everything, even matters of the heart, certainly past the externals. Second, he knew that God is a holy God. Third, he understood that God is going to hold people accountable, that there would be a day of reckoning. Finally, he knew that God is merciful, so he cast himself before Him.

3 What contrasts do you see between how these two men viewed God?

How did each man's view of God impact the way he prayed?

4 What is one characteristic of God that helps shape the way you pray, and how does meditating on this attribute keep your prayers God-centered and healthy?

Read Snapshot "Prayer Reveals How You See Yourself"

PRAYER REVEALS HOW YOU SEE YOURSELF

The Pharisee. What does the Pharisee's prayer reveal about how he viewed himself? The first thing it reveals is that he was totally deceived about his own morality. Jeremiah 17:9 says, "The heart is deceitful above all things and beyond cure. Who can understand it?" Sadly, the Pharisee didn't have a clue about what was really going on in his own heart and life. He saw himself as a holy man, yet he was far from that. He was also deceived about the source of his justification. He thought "good works" would suffice in pleasing God, and he was fairly confident he had done plenty of them.

The Tax Collector. What does the tax collector's prayer reveal about how he viewed himself? He called himself "a sinner" and knew that he was incapable of changing his condition, that self-justification was a waste of time. But he also knew God valued him enough to offer mercy. He was not degrading himself; he was merely being honest. He saw himself as a candidate for forgiveness, so he threw himself on God's mercies, trusting that God would deliver him.

---

5 What contrasts do you see between how these two men viewed themselves?

How did each man's view of himself impact the way he prayed?

6 In what ways can Christians today see themselves in the wrong light and end up praying like the Pharisee?

Read Snapshot "Prayer Reveals How You See Others"

PRAYER REVEALS HOW YOU SEE OTHERS

The Pharisee. What does the Pharisee's prayer reveal about how he viewed others? In a word, he felt contempt. His attitude toward the tax collector was, "You are despicable, a loser, a rotten sinner." As such, the Pharisee was confident God had as much disdain for the tax collector as he did, certainly that the man was unworthy of God's grace. Bottom line, the Pharisee lived with a sense of spiritual hierarchy, sure that he was high up the ladder and the tax collector was many rungs down.

The Tax Collector. What does the tax collector's prayer reveal about his view of others? You might say, "His prayer doesn't reveal anything. There is no mention of others in it." But, doesn't the absence of any mention of other people teach us something? Might it not teach us that from time to time it is appropriate to forget about others, shut out the world, and get alone with God? The tax collector in Jesus' story knew this was a time to humble himself before God and do business with His maker.

---

7 Certainly there are times when we need to prayerfully lift up the needs of others. But there are also times when we should come before God for a one-on-one, heart-to-heart conversation. Why is it important to regularly meet with God alone, "forgetting the world," as it were?

The Pharisee offered his prayer with one eye open, looking at the people around him (particularly the tax collector). What are some dangers of comparing ourselves to others as we pray?

8 According to the Luke 18 passage, what were the results of these two prayers, and why did they lead these men to such different places?

Read Snapshot "Helpful Prayer Tips"

HELPFUL PRAYER TIPS

Consider the following ideas and tips as you seek to grow in your communication with God through prayer:

The Posture of Prayer. At times, getting on our knees or flat on our faces is absolutely appropriate. When we bow or kneel before God, this physical act can help move our hearts to a place of declaring, "God, You are holy. I don't deserve to lift my eyes up to heaven." Sometimes we can physically bow and get on our knees. We can also bow our head and our heart. The key is that a posture of submission, outward or inward, can help us come before God with a yielded humility.

Pause Before Praying. If we pause before praying to really think about what we are doing and to whom we are speaking, this will keep us from shifting into autopilot mode and speaking a bunch of mindless words. Whether we are alone or in a group, we can briefly quiet our heart at the start, asking God to help us to pray thoughtfully.

Content Evaluation. As we honestly answer the question, "Is there a good balance in my prayers?" we can protect ourselves from spending all of our time asking for things and never confessing or thanking God. I encourage people to use the simple word "ACTS" to help them lift up balanced prayers. Each letter reminds us of an important aspect of prayer:

- **A**doration: Lift up prayers praising God for who He is, His attributes and nature.
- **C**onfession: Admit your sins, mistakes, and hidden struggles to God and ask for His grace.
- **T**hanksgiving: Thank God for the things He has done and for His provision.
- **S**upplication: Lift your needs and the needs of others before God.

Use Variety. We can do our best to avoid getting into a prayer rut. For a time we might want to pray through the psalms, using them as a launch pad into conversation with God. At another time we might want to write out our prayers or use the ACTS structure to direct our prayers. We might want to lift our prayers in community — with a friend or family member — to see how this grows our communication with God. As we remain open to try new things, we help keep prayer fresh.

9 What is one way you pray that really connects you to God? How might others use this approach to prayer to broaden and deepen their communication with God?

PUTTING YOURSELF IN THE PICTURE

Try Something New

Use one of the prayer ideas discussed in this session or recommended by one of your group members to see if it connects for you. Be sure to try an approach to prayer that is new for you and that stretches you.

SELF-EVALUATION

In the coming week, try to be conscious about your own prayers. Don't grill yourself, but just notice how you pray. Write down some reflections around these three questions:

- What do my prayers reveal about my view of God?

- What do my prayers reveal about how I view myself?

- What do my prayers say about how I view others?

AREN'T ALL RELIGIONS THE SAME?

REFLECTIONS FROM SESSION 5

1. How have you been encouraged to reflect on your prayer life since your last group gathering?
2. If you have experienced an answer to prayer in the past couple of weeks, tell your group about it.

THE BIG PICTURE

There was a day when people going to the store to buy a bar of soap had it easy ... there were only one or two options. Today you can spend an hour trying to make a decision. Yes, there are many brands to pick from, but it is even more complex. Do I want a bar of soap or a bottle of liquid hand soap? If I decide on liquid, I have a plethora of scent options. Once I choose the "Ocean Scent" fragrance, I have to decide if I want a plain bottle or if I want to pay a little more for the decorative bottle with pictures of sea horses on it. Such are the dilemmas in a world with a proliferation of options ... and most of us like it that way.

Besides, in the vast majority of situations, our decision comes down to a matter of personal preference. Rarely is it about right and wrong. Choosing a bar or bottle of soap is not a moral issue, nor is our Starbucks order, the brand of jeans we buy, or the make of car that suits us best.

Some years ago the major soft drink companies battled each other with taste tests to determine which was the best. Of course, there is no right or wrong (as much as soft drink manufacturers would like you to think so). One person likes Coke and another enjoys the taste of Pepsi. Both are carbonated water, sugar, and flavoring. It is about personal taste.

Isn't this also the case with world religions? Aren't the various religious expressions really like soap options, car model preferences, or soft drinks? When it comes right down to it, aren't religions really saying the same thing but with different scents and packaging? Is it fair to look at religions like a spiritual taste test where we line them up, take a sample, and then choose which one works for us? Or is there something more going on here?

A WIDE ANGLE VIEW

1 How have you seen the options in life increase over the past decade, and how has this impacted the way people tend to see the world?

Many people see the various world religions as basically saying the same thing. Choosing one is just a matter of personal preference. What do you think about this attitude?

A BIBLICAL PORTRAIT

Read Acts 17:16–34 and John 14:1–7

2 If Jesus and the apostle Paul were sitting on a modern-day panel that was discussing world religions, how do you think they would respond to *one* of these statements:

- All of the world religions are really saying the same thing.

- Every religion is equally valid and true.

- The Bible never claims that Jesus or the Christian faith have a corner on the truth.

- Jesus never claimed to be the exclusive way to heaven.

SHARPENING THE FOCUS

Read Snapshot "All Religions Are the Same . . . This Belief Is Illogical"

ALL RELIGIONS ARE THE SAME . . . THIS BELIEF IS ILLOGICAL

In an effort to help the congregation of Willow Creek understand the beliefs of the major world religions and the uniqueness of the Christian faith, we invited a panel of leaders of Buddhism, Islam, Hinduism, Judaism, and Christianity to speak at one of our services. We asked them a series of questions and let them speak for themselves and their faith perspective.

One thing that became immediately obvious was that the various world religions hold beliefs diametrically opposed to each other. In some cases, it became crystal-clear that there is no way a logical and clear-thinking person could say that all religions are the same. For example, Christianity, Judaism, and Islam believe in one God. These religions are monotheistic. Buddhism believes in many gods . . . it is polytheistic. Hinduism, in a sense, does not believe in any god at all. So, I ask, is it possible that there could be only one God and equally true that there are many gods and equally true that there is no personal being we can call God? No! If there is only one God, it is logically inconsistent to say that there are many gods.

In a similar way, Christianity teaches that Jesus Christ came as God in human flesh and that He is the only true Savior. Jesus, and only Jesus, can cleanse us from sin and give us the hope of heaven. Judaism and Islam reject the idea that Jesus was God incarnate and the Savior of the world. Is it possible that Jesus came as God incarnate and equally true that Jesus was not fully divine? These two claims are mutually exclusive and only one of them can be true. If one is true, the other must be false.

When it comes to religious beliefs, some people feel comfortable checking their minds at the door. They will say things like, "All religions are really saying the same thing," without looking closely to discover that they make dramatically different claims. They will also say, "All religions are equally true and valid," without looking close enough to see that many religions make claims that are mutually exclusive. It is simply illogical to say that all religions are the same and are equally true.

3 Why do you think people who are logical about many other areas of life are comfortable saying, "All religions are the same and equally true," when this is an illogical statement?

4 What are some claims of the Christian faith that are diametrically opposed to the teachings of other faith systems?

Read Snapshot "All Religions Are the Same . . . This Belief Is an Insult to Other Religions"

ALL RELIGIONS ARE THE SAME . . . THIS BELIEF IS AN INSULT TO OTHER RELIGIONS

 In an effort to be diplomatic and "kind," it has become popular to say that all religions are really the same or agree on nearly everything. But, if you think about it, such a declaration is highly insulting to devout members of any faith system.

Imagine sitting down with a deeply committed Jew and a devout Muslim and you begin the conversation by saying, "Guess what, both of you really believe the same things, you just don't know it! The truth is, about 99 percent of your beliefs are the same." I doubt these people would agree. When we brought leaders from the five major world religions to Willow Creek, the panelists were all polite and respectful of each other, but they disagreed on many things, including most doctrinal issues. It is tremendously arrogant and insulting to tell devout adherents of various religions that all their beliefs are the same.

---

5 Respond to *one* of these statements:

- Claiming that all world religions are the same reveals significant ignorance about the world religions.

- Claiming that all religions are basically the same would be insulting to any religious person who is devout and serious about their faith.

Read Snapshot "All Religions Are the Same ... This Belief Is Contrary to the Life and Teaching of Jesus"

ALL RELIGIONS ARE THE SAME ... THIS BELIEF IS CONTRARY TO THE LIFE AND TEACHING OF JESUS

Jesus lived in a pluralistic world. As a matter of fact, it would be fair to say that the world had as much or more religious diversity in the first century as it does today. But Jesus was still comfortable lifting up Himself as the Messiah, the fulfillment of Old Testament prophecy, God in human flesh, and the only way to an eternal relationship with the Father. These bold proclamations were either the babblings of a madman or the truth from God.

To say that all religions are the same is to undercut the unique claims of Jesus. It is to water down the gospel that led Jesus to the cross. Jesus did not leave this option open to us. His claims were so clear and strong that we can't get around them.

6 If Jesus came to bring love and grace to the world, why would He make claims that could divide people and draw distinctions between Himself and the teachings of other religious leaders throughout history?

What are examples of things Jesus taught that actually drew a line and caused division?

Read Snapshot "All Religions Are the Same ... This Belief Is
Opposed to the Teaching of the Bible"

ALL RELIGIONS ARE THE SAME ... THIS BELIEF IS
OPPOSED TO THE TEACHING OF THE BIBLE

Not only did Jesus teach that He was the only way to heaven and the unique Son of God, but all through the Bible is a thread of teaching that lifts up the God of the Bible as the only true God. In Old Testament times Yahweh, the God of Israel, claimed not only the supreme place but declared that the gods of the other nations were really just idols and had no existence (1 Chron. 16:26). The Old Testament teaches that only the one true God should be worshiped (Ex. 20:3–6). This truth was so important that it makes up the first two of the Ten Commandments.

Any time the people of God embraced other "gods" and worshiped idols, they came under severe discipline. This very sin led to the complete decline of the Northern Kingdom of Israel. Nothing in the teaching of the Bible leaves room for an attitude that says, "All religious expressions are equally true or valid." As a matter of fact, the Bible consistently teaches that there is one God, Yahweh. Worship of any other "god" or idol was strictly forbidden.

7

Why do you think God is so concerned that people not
embrace other religious systems?

Read Snapshot "All Religions Are the Same ... This Belief
Endangers People"

ALL RELIGIONS ARE THE SAME ...
THIS BELIEF ENDANGERS PEOPLE

In an effort to be inclusive, kind, and politically correct, many people today want to be diplomatic and say that all religious pathways lead to heaven. Christians who declare that Jesus is the only way to an eternal relationship with the Father and that those without Him are lost and separated from God are considered arrogant, narrow, or closed-minded. They may be called "unloving," perhaps even marginalized.

Here is the dilemma. If Christians remain silent because we never want to offend anyone, who will tell the story of Jesus to those who are still wandering like sheep without a shepherd? If we buy the conventional wisdom that says, "All religions are really the same," we will have no reason to fulfill the Great Commission, in which Jesus said, "Therefore go and make disciples of all nations, baptizing them in the name of the Father and of the Son and of the Holy Spirit, and teaching them to obey everything I have commanded you" (Matt. 28:19–20).

8

How is God's strong call to worship Him, and Him alone, a sign of His love for human beings?

9

Tell about one person you know and care about who is not a follower of Jesus.

What can you do to share the love and message of God with this person and point him or her toward Jesus, the Savior?

PUTTING YOURSELF IN THE PICTURE

HELPFUL REMINDERS

Take time during the next week to read the "I am" sayings of Jesus as well as some other claims He made. Let these unique claims of Jesus, all recorded in the gospel of John, be clear reminders of who Jesus is:

- 4:25–26

- 6:35

- 8:12

- 8:23–24

- 8:58

- 9:5

- 10:7–10

- 10:11–15

- 10:36

- 11:25

- 12:32

- 14:1–3

- 14:6

- 15:5

- 17:20–21

- 18:37

- 20:21–23

PRAYER FOR YOURSELF AND OTHERS

In the coming days, pray in two very specific directions:

- Ask God to give you grace-filled boldness to hold to your faith and share it with others. Pray that you will never acquiesce to the pressures of the world and compromise your faith in Jesus.
- Pray for opportunities to serve people who are not followers of Jesus. Ask God to give you open doors to share your story of faith.

LEADER'S NOTES

Leading a Bible discussion—especially for the first time—can make you feel both nervous and excited. If you are nervous, realize that you are in good company. Many biblical leaders, such as Moses, Joshua, and the apostle Paul, felt nervous and inadequate to lead others (see, for example, 1 Cor. 2:3). Yet God's grace was sufficient for them, just as it will be for you.

Some excitement is also natural. Your leadership is a gift to the others in the group. Keep in mind, however, that other group members also share responsibility for the group. Your role is simply to stimulate discussion by asking questions and encouraging people to respond. The suggestions listed below can help you to be an effective leader.

PREPARING TO LEAD

1. Ask God to help you understand and apply the passage to your own life. Unless that happens, you will not be prepared to lead others.
2. Carefully work through each question in the study guide. Meditate and reflect on the passage as you formulate your answers.
3. Familiarize yourself with the Leader's Notes for each session. These will help you understand the purpose of the session and will provide valuable information about the questions in the session. The Leader's Notes are not intended to be read to the group. These notes are primarily for your use as a group leader and for your preparation. However, when you find a section that relates well to your group, you may want to read a brief portion or encourage them to read this section at another time.
4. Pray for the various members of the group. Ask God to use these sessions to make you better disciples of Jesus Christ.
5. Before the first session, make sure each person has a study guide. Encourage them to prepare beforehand for each session.

LEADING THE SESSION

1. Begin the session on time. If people realize that the session begins on schedule, they will work harder to arrive on time.

2. At the beginning of your first time together, explain that these sessions are designed to be discussions, not lectures. Encourage everyone to participate, but realize some may be hesitant to speak during the first few sessions.

3. Don't be afraid of silence. People in the group may need time to think before responding.

4. Avoid answering your own questions. If necessary, rephrase a question until it is clearly understood. Even an eager group will quickly become passive and silent if they think the leader will do most of the talking.

5. Encourage more than one answer to each question. Ask, "What do the rest of you think?" or "Anyone else?" until several people have had a chance to respond.

6. Try to be affirming whenever possible. Let people know you appreciate their insights into the passage.

7. Never reject an answer. If it is clearly wrong, ask, "Which verse led you to that conclusion?" Or let the group handle the problem by asking them what they think about the question.

8. Avoid going off on tangents. If people wander off course, gently bring them back to the passage being considered.

9. Conclude your time together with conversational prayer. Ask God to help you apply those things that you learned in the session.

10. End on time. This will be easier if you control the pace of the discussion by not spending too much time on some questions or too little on others.

We encourage all small group leaders to use *Leading Life-Changing Small Groups* (Zondervan) by Bill Donahue and the Willow Creek Small Group Team while leading their group. Developed and used by Willow Creek Community Church, this guide is an excellent resource for training and equipping followers of Christ to effectively lead small groups. It includes valuable information on how to utilize fun and creative relationship-building exercises for your group; how to plan your meeting; how to share the leadership load by identifying, developing, and working with an "apprentice leader"; and how to find creative ways to do group prayer. In addition, the book includes material and tips on handling potential conflicts and difficult personalities, forming group covenants, inviting new members, improving listening skills, studying the Bible, and much more. Using *Leading Life-Changing Small Groups* will help you create a group that members love to be a part of.

Now let's discuss the different elements of this small group study guide and how to use them for the session portion of your group meeting.

THE BIG PICTURE

Each session will begin with a short story or overview of the lesson theme. This is called "The Big Picture" because it introduces the central theme of the session. You will need to read this section as a group or have group members read it on their own before discussion begins. Here are three ways you can approach this section of the small group session:

- As the group leader, read this section out loud for the whole group and then move into the questions in the next section, "A Wide Angle View." (You might read the first week, but then use the other two options below to encourage group involvement.)
- Ask a group member to volunteer to read this section for the group. This allows another group member to participate. It is best to ask someone in advance to give them time to read over the section before reading it to the group. It is also good to ask someone to volunteer, and not to assign this task. Some people do not feel comfortable reading in front of a group. After a group member has read this section out loud, move into the discussion questions.
- Allow time at the beginning of the session for each person to read this section silently. If you do this, be sure to allow enough time for everyone to finish reading so they can think about what they've read and be ready for meaningful discussion.

A WIDE ANGLE VIEW

This section includes one or more questions that move the group into a general discussion of the session topic. These questions are designed to help group members begin discussing the topic in an open and honest manner. Once the topic of the lesson has been established, move on to the Bible passage for the session.

A BIBLICAL PORTRAIT

This portion of the session includes a Scripture reading and one or more questions that help group members see how the theme of the session is rooted and based in biblical teaching. The Scripture reading can be handled just like "The Big Picture" section:

You can read it for the group, have a group member read it, or allow time for silent reading. Make sure everyone has a Bible or that you have Bibles available for those who need them. Once you have read the passage, ask the question(s) in this section so that group members can dig into the truth of the Bible.

SHARPENING THE FOCUS

The majority of the discussion questions for the session are in this section. These questions are practical and help group members apply biblical teaching to their daily lives.

SNAPSHOTS

The "Snapshots" in each session help prepare group members for discussion. These anecdotes give additional insight to the topic being discussed. Each "Snapshot" should be read at a designated point in the session. This is clearly marked in the session as well as in the Leader's Notes. Again, follow the same format as you do with "The Big Picture" section and the "Biblical Portrait" section: Either you read the anecdote, have a group member volunteer to read, or provide time for silent reading. However you approach this section, you will find these anecdotes very helpful in triggering lively dialogue and moving discussion in a meaningful direction.

PUTTING YOURSELF IN THE PICTURE

Here's where you roll up your sleeves and put the truth into action. This portion is very practical and action-oriented. At the end of each session there will be suggestions for one or two ways group members can put what they've just learned into practice. Review the action goals at the end of each session and challenge group members to work on one or more of them in the coming week.

You will find follow-up questions for the "Putting Yourself in the Picture" section at the beginning of the next week's session. Starting with the second week, there will be time set aside at the beginning of the session to look back and talk about how you have tried to apply God's Word in your life since your last time together.

PRAYER

You will want to open and close your small group with a time of prayer. Occasionally, there will be specific direction within a session for how you can do this. Most of the time, however, you will need to decide the best place to stop and pray. You may want to pray or have a group member volunteer to begin the lesson with a prayer. Or you might want to read "The Big Picture" and discuss the "Wide Angle View" questions before opening in prayer. In some cases, it might be best to open in prayer after you have read the Bible passage. You need to decide where you feel an opening prayer best fits for your group.

When opening in prayer, think in terms of the session theme and pray for group members (including yourself) to be responsive to the truth of Scripture and the working of the Holy Spirit. If you have seekers in your group (people investigating Christianity but not yet believers), be sensitive to your expectations for group prayer. Seekers may not yet be ready to take part in group prayer.

Be sure to close your group with a time of prayer as well. One option is for you to pray for the entire group. Or you might allow time for group members to offer audible prayers that others can agree with in their hearts. Another approach would be to allow a time of silence for one-on-one prayers with God and then to close this time with a simple "Amen."

HOW DO WE FIND PEACE IN A WAR-TORN WORLD?

ISAIAH 9:6–7; LUKE 2:14; MATTHEW 5:9; JOHN 14:25–27; ACTS 10:34–36

INTRODUCTION

Romans 12:18 tells Christ-followers: "If it is possible, as far as it depends on you, live at peace with everyone." Yet the evil one's strategy to sow seeds of strife throughout society seems to be working rather well. From immediate family to international structures, individuals and world leaders are often all too quick to want to settle differences in other-than-peaceful ways. This session focuses on the steps we can take to become peacemakers in a war-torn world. There is an old song that says, "Let there be peace on earth, and let it begin with me." In this session we will look at our part in bringing peace to a world that desperately needs it.

THE BIG PICTURE

Take time to read this introduction with the group. There are suggestions for how this can be done in the beginning of the leader's section.

A WIDE ANGLE VIEW

Question One This session and opening question can be very tricky. Responses to this question just might set the tone for your whole group time. As a leader, be vulnerable, perhaps sharing briefly about a relationship conflict of your own. If group members will enter in and be honest with each other, this could be a powerful discussion. The key will be learning for ourselves and not looking at this as a good lesson for someone else.

Another dynamic in this session is that all stories need to be told without names or other identifying details. We never want a small group study to become a gossip session. The Bible is clear that gossip is a sin. So, lay down these important ground rules for the group from the very start.

A BIBLICAL PORTRAIT

Read Isaiah 9:6–7; Luke 2:14; Matthew 5:9; John 14:25–27; and Acts 10:34–36 (all are printed in the session)

Question Two Peace is not a side note for Jesus … it is a central concern. Jesus teaches about peace with God and peace with each other, and identifies Himself as the bringer of peace. The passages listed before this question present the full scope — past, present, and future — of this truth: Jesus was about peace even before He entered human history, He came to bring peace, and as the resurrected Lord He will help us seek peace.

We could never be at peace with God except for the sacrifice of Jesus and His reconciling work. We would never have the strength to seek peace with other people if it were not for Jesus, the Prince of Peace.

SHARPENING THE FOCUS

Read Snapshot "The Ultimate Warmonger" before Question 4

Question Four One of the reasons war, conflict, and relational brokenness will always be part of this life is that the enemy of our souls spends so much time seeking to destroy relationships. If we look closely at history, and our own personal journey through life, we can quickly see that his tactics are very effective.

Peter says, "Be alert!" Satan is like a lion, prowling around. We have all seen documentaries of lions on the prowl in Africa. They crawl low to the ground … silent, their legs coiled like springs, ready to pounce. Those who want to stay alive keep on their guard, watching for any sudden movement in the brush or a flash of golden fur. In the same way, followers of Jesus know that we can never drop our guard when it comes to our relational life. If we do, marriages are attacked, church community is compromised, friendships spin upside-down, and even small groups can become conflicted. We have to be ever vigilant and aware of the tactics of the ultimate warmonger.

Read Snapshot "Deal with It" before Question 5

Question Five Jesus leaves no room for His followers to bury their head in the sand like the proverbial ostrich. When we recognize conflict in our relationships we are called to deal with it. We are to go directly to the person, not telling other people about how we have been wronged. We also need to be very careful that we don't spiritualize gossip or slander by dressing it up as a prayer need. Some people go to friends and ask them to pray for the situation, being sure they communicate how they have been wronged. This is sin! We are to go directly to the person and seek reconciliation.

Read Snapshot "Walk Out of a Worship Service" before Question 7

Question Seven When we gather for corporate worship, the Holy Spirit is always present and at work. These moments are ripe for the Spirit to convict and call us to repentance. Whether this happens during a song, time of prayer, or the message, we ought to act; to actually get up as discreetly as possible, slip out, and make a call to the person with whom we need to be reconciled. If they don't answer, leave a message. Tell them we want to talk.

If someone in the church or even the pastor asks us why we had to slip out, let's be honest and explain that the Holy Spirit convicted us of a relationship that needed healing and we were acting on it, just as Jesus taught. We don't need to give details or a name, but we can ask them to pray for us as we seek to honor God by seeking peace in this relationship.

Read Snapshot "Commit to Peace" before Question 8

Question Eight The key here is that we do our part. That's all we can do. If we seek peace in the relationship and the other person refuses, we should no longer live with the weight of the situation. If we have told the other person that the door of our heart is open to reconcile whenever they are ready, then we can feel peace with God and peace in our own heart.

Read Snapshot "Will Wars Ever Cease?" before Question 9

Question Nine The Bible is hope-filled and optimistic, not negative or fatalistic. But God's Word is also honest about some things that are simply part of this world. For instance, Jesus said, "The poor you will always have with you" (Matt. 26:11). He was not saying poverty is good or right, simply that it is part of a sinful, broken world. Jesus actually calls us to care for the poor, and throughout the Old and New Testaments the call to give to and care for the marginalized is loud and clear. But poverty will never be banished from the earth until Jesus comes again.

The Bible deals with the topic of war in this same sense. God longs for peace and He calls us to be His agents of peace. But war will be part of the human experience as long as sin is in the world.

PUTTING YOURSELF IN THE PICTURE

Challenge group members to take time in the coming week to use part or all of this application section as an opportunity for continued growth.

CAN OUR PLANET SURVIVE?

GENESIS 1; PSALM 24:1—2

INTRODUCTION

God has given us a pretty amazing planet on which to live. But over time, the effects of progress and man's desire for convenience have begun to wear negatively on our Father's world. Those disproportionately affected by abuse of resources and pollution of the earth are the poor. This session reiterates what God expects from us in the care of this planet—His planet—and suggests ways we can start making a difference in caring for it. One important part of this process is to identify God as the Creator and His creation as a good gift.

THE BIG PICTURE

Take time to read this introduction with the group. There are suggestions for how this can be done in the beginning of the leader's section.

A WIDE ANGLE VIEW

Question One We are all offenders, small and large, when it comes to abusing creation. Take time as a group to be honest about how society has fallen short of caring for the earth. But look honestly on a personal level as well. It is easy to point a finger at a group or nation. It is hard to point a finger at ourselves. Where have each of us missed the mark when it comes to being good stewards of the earth?

A BIBLICAL PORTRAIT

Read Genesis 1 and Psalm 24:1–2

Question Two Just as we can discover things about an artist when we look at their sculpture, painting, or poem, we learn about God when we view His handiwork in creation. Look up at the stars and be amazed at the extravagance of God as you realize you can't begin to count all the luminaries in the night sky. Walk an Irish hillside and discover that God loves texture and color ... you will see more shades of green than you knew existed. Peer down at the water in a Caribbean lagoon and see shades of blue you might not see anywhere else. From the order to the beauty of creation, God reveals so much about His nature and character.

Question Three God is clearly concerned about His creation. He made it. He declared it, "Very good." He calls us to care for it, to work it, and to treat it as He would. With this in mind, we should be stirred to take stewardship of the environment very seriously. From fighting pollution to preserving resources (or any other action that honors what God has made), Christians should be concerned and engaged.

SHARPENING THE FOCUS

Read Snapshot "Subdue, Rule, Work, and Care" before Question 4

Question Four God calls His people to engage with creation in a number of ways. The two that are often misunderstood are *to subdue* and *to rule*.

Subdue. A few years ago at a Leadership Summit a woman got out of her seat and started down the aisle during my final message. I could tell she was headed onto the stage. We have security people in every one of our public services, and I was confident that they would intercept her. Just before she got to the stage, sure enough, one of our people slipped out of a row, kindly put his arm around her, and subdued her. He did not manhandle her, tackle her to the ground, or zap her with a taser. He didn't mistreat her in any way. All he did was bring her into conformity with the behavioral standards of the event. He walked her into the lobby and calmed her down.

After the event, I had a chance to interact via email with this woman, who told me her medication had caused an imbalance and she profusely apologized. I was so thankful that the security guy only subdued her; nothing more. That's the idea of this imperative in Genesis. God says that whatever gets unruly — if vines overgrow the pathways, if trees require trimming — that it should be subdued, brought under control.

Rule. Scripture tells parents to rule over their children. This simply means that they are to bring them into orderliness, to provide them with safety, to consistently develop them over a long period of time. The New Testament adds this warning (my paraphrase): "Parents, you better not rule over your kids in an abusive way. You'll incite rebellion, and they'll hate you." It's the same idea in Genesis. We're to have authority over the earth, but not in an abusive kind of way.

Read Snapshot "Creation Gives Witness to God" before Question 6

Question Six I was on a sailboat once with a friend who was quite cynical about the existence of God—and it happened to be right about the time of a spectacular sunset. I had been talking with this man for years about Christ and the existence of God but he had remained strong in his resistance. That evening I just worked up the boldness and said to him, "Now you look at this sunset and the beauty of this water that guys like you and me love to sail on, and you tell me this all just happened. Are you telling me that that's a cosmic accident? All of this?"

He was silent for about thirty seconds, just looking at the sunset. Finally he said, "Yeah, you're right." I said, "Well, let's talk about that God, because He loves you." It wasn't long thereafter that my friend committed himself to Christ and he has been walking with Him ever since. It was a moment looking at a sunset, the work of the Master Artist, which changed his inner world. That is when he started to open up himself to God.

Read Snapshot "Creation Gives Us Places to Connect with God" before Question 7

Question Seven God's creative realm has intrinsic value, but it also adds value to our lives in some unexpected ways. It sets the context for defining moments; it calms our spirits; it stimulates creativity; it increases our faith. I can remember a time I stood in front of one particular range of the Rocky Mountains and could not help but be reminded how our God is as solid as a rock and He can move mountains.

Jesus had a practice of meeting with the Father in places saturated in creative beauty. He loved the seaside, the hills, and even the quiet of the desert. We need to learn from the Master and take advantage of the many ways we can draw near to God in creation.

Read Snapshot "The Bad News and the Good News" before Question 8

Question Eight A groundswell of people today are saying, "We need to care for the earth and turn around the cycle of environmental abuse." Some are motivated by spiritual values.

Some just understand intellectually that we cannot continue to abuse the place where we live; it's the only planet we have. Some are motivated by God's call, and others are just motivated by good old common sense and a true concern for the world. These days the two groups are starting to get together, and some interesting change is going on.

If someone is committed to caring for the earth, we can seek ways to partner with them. Who knows, maybe as we work together to steward and protect the earth, we will have a chance to tell them about the Creator who made all things and who loves them.

Putting Yourself in the Picture

Challenge group members to take time in the coming week to use part or all of this application section as an opportunity for continued growth.

How Do I Balance Life's Demands?

Ecclesiastes 3:1–8; Isaiah 30:15–16

Introduction

We live in a world where busyness is a badge of honor. "We are driven" could be our motto. Even children are experiencing stress from the pressures of life. Into our fast-paced lives God speaks, calling us to slow down, find peace, and strike a balance among all the demands each day holds. If we are going to nurture and grow our souls, it will mean learning to slow down. In this session we will look at some practical steps we can take to restore balance in our lives as we seek to tend to our souls.

The Big Picture

Take time to read this introduction with the group. There are suggestions for how this can be done in the beginning of the leader's section.

A Wide Angle View

Question One Most of us feel the stress of expectations, the pressure of full schedules, and the tension that comes with seeking to establish balance among the busyness of life. Yet we want to experience peace of heart and growth in our souls. As you begin this session, invite group members to be honest about both the challenge of full schedules and also the ways they have experienced spiritual growth when they have slowed down and established balance in their lives.

A Biblical Portrait

Read Ecclesiastes 3:1–8 and Isaiah 30:15–16

Question Two Ecclesiastes tells us that there is time for everything that matters. In light of this fact, we should live with the conviction that we can make time for our soul, for rich relationships, and for connecting with God. Isaiah paints a picture of how God invites us to rest and quietness, but how we often choose to rush and race instead. We need to learn from Scripture and choose to take time for the things in life that matter most.

SHARPENING THE FOCUS

Read Snapshot "Speed Versus Soul" before Question 3

Question Three People who study time management and stress have identified a number of reasons we run so fast in our modern-day world. One that they mention frequently is the sheer volume of positive, exciting, entertaining, and developmental opportunities available to the average person today.

As a kid growing up in Kalamazoo, Michigan, in the 1950s, entire months went by when there was not a single extracurricular activity available to my friends and me. There weren't six different soccer leagues and five basketball programs running year-round. Indoor video arcades and mega shopping malls did not exist. We had one black-and-white television in our home—and it had lousy reception. There was no cable, no DVDs, and no video game systems. All seven of our family members sat down at 6:00 p.m. every evening and had dinner together. During the middle of that unhurried dinner, my dad would reach into the red cabinet next to the table and pull out a Bible. He would read it to our family, in no particular hurry. This was only a few decades ago.

If you jump ahead to today, the potential involvement opportunities for kids and families has exploded. Some high-energy kids want to be involved in all of them, especially if their friends are participating. And good-hearted parents can't bear the thought of depriving their children of anything that could add color and texture and value to their lives. Before you know it, kids are way overcommitted. They're anxious and tired.

At some point we must ask the question: Does every opportunity have to be engaged in? At what point do multiple opportunities become wolves in sheep's clothing because they speed up our lives to the point where the inner person gets extinguished?

Add the passion for competition and increased stimulation due to high-tech toys and we have a generation of children, youth, and adults who might lose their souls if they are not careful.

Read Snapshot "Just Say No" before Question 4

Question Four Saying no takes practice. But if we work at it, we can become very good at it. We need to be kind and smile *when* we say it. In some situations we might need to explain *why* we are saying it. (For example: "That sounds like a wonderful opportunity, it really does. But my schedule is full and I am seeking to establish balance in my life. If I say yes, I will be overextended, and I have made a commitment to not do that anymore.") If we are talking with another Christian, we might even tell them about what we learned in this session and explain how we are learning to say no as we seek to grow our soul and establish balance in our life.

Read Snapshot "You Win" before Question 6

Question Six From childhood to adulthood, competition is becoming more and more a part of the fabric of our society. Children deal with academic and athletic competition at younger and younger ages. Adults face increasing competition in the marketplace. This mentality leads to health issues (ulcers, stress-related illnesses, etc.). It can affect our relational world; we forget that the people in our lives are just that, people, not an obstacle to overcome. An overly competitive spirit also can create emotional turmoil as we spend an inordinate amount of energy trying to win.

Read Snapshot "Sensory Control" before Questions 8 & 9

Questions Eight and Nine The key to this exercise and follow-up question is honesty. Invite group members to take time to really reflect on where they are on this scale. Then make space to talk together about ways you can establish a healthy balance of quiet and sensory-laden activities.

Putting Yourself in the Picture

Challenge group members to take time in the coming week to use part or all of this application section as an opportunity for continued growth.

IS GOD REALLY OUT THERE?

PSALM 19:1—6; PSALM 8:1—9; ROMANS 1:20; GENESIS 1:1—5

INTRODUCTION

We all have people in our lives who are not yet sure God is out there. They might be apathetic about spiritual things or seriously seeking. In this session we will look at four different ways we can help these people move forward on their spiritual journey. Though not an exhaustive list, the ideas presented are great ways for each group member to initiate meaningful spiritual conversations.

THE BIG PICTURE

Take time to read this introduction with the group. There are suggestions for how this can be done in the beginning of the leader's section.

A WIDE ANGLE VIEW

Question One Some people meet God on the water. Oceans, lakes, and rivers draw them into the presence of the Creator. Others see God's power and majesty in the magnificence of the mountains. Yet others find the heat and silence of the desert most conducive to drawing them into the presence of God. Take time as a group to tell about where each person connects with God.

A BIBLICAL PORTRAIT

Read Psalm 19:1–6; Psalm 8:1–9; Romans 1:20; and Genesis 1:1–5

Question Two These passages communicate a number of connections between God and His creation. But it is important to note that God is the Creator, but still separate from creation. Pantheism says that all things are God and God is all things. This is not the teaching of the Bible. God is the Creator of all that we see, but the creation itself is not divine.

God is the maker of heaven and earth. He spoke all things into existence. He sustains all things. Creation points to Him as a piece of art points to the artist. The heavens declare the glory and character of God. But they are not God.

Question Three Just as when we look at a beautiful painting or sculpture, we learn something about the artist, the majesty and beauty of creation teach us about the nature of God. God loves variety, color, texture, and diversity. The wonderful breadth of places, creatures, and people declare His majesty. In addition, the complex design of everything from galaxies to a single cell point to the Creator's intentionality and sense of order.

Sharpening the Focus

Read Snapshot "Intelligent Design" before Question 4

Question Four When I am talking with a person unsure of God's existence I'll sometimes quote the infamous Charles Darwin, unofficial father of evolutionary theory, who after studying the human eye wrote in his book *The Origin of Species*, "To suppose that the human eye, with so many parts all working together, could have been formed by natural selection seems, I freely confess, absurd in the highest degree." Even Darwin knew that it makes no sense to think that the complexity of the human eye came about by accident.

This argument from complexity, formally called the *teleological argument*, has long been used to help people wrestle with the existence of God. It simply asks the question, "Who or what is responsible for the intricacies, symmetry, order, and marvels we see all around us in the natural realm?"

The philosopher William Paley wrote, "There cannot be a design without a designer. There cannot be contrivance without a contriver. There cannot be order, anywhere, without choice." In modern parlance Paley is saying, "Reasonable people look at a wristwatch and they wonder which company made it. Reasonable people look at a laptop computer and check to see if IBM, Apple, or Dell manufactured it. Reasonable people look at an airliner and wonder if it was made by Boeing or Airbus." Paley questioned why reasonable people would look at a human eye, an orchid in bloom, or an eagle in flight and believe that each of these marvels is the consequence of a random accident, an inexplicable explosion in outer space that no one can intelligently describe or verify.

Read Snapshot "Moral Oughtness" before Question 5

Question Five Sometimes I ask my seeking friends to ponder the question of "moral oughtness" quietly and deeply. I'll ask, "If human beings are only semi-advanced apes, who themselves evolved from slimy pond creatures that somehow formed out of misty gases a billion years ago, how is it that human beings everywhere operate with a sense of moral oughtness? What, other than the work of a supreme moral being, accounts for that?" And I'll say, "Do you have an answer?"

Esteemed British author C. S. Lewis wrote on this subject more compellingly than anyone in history. In his book *Mere Christianity* he concludes, "The universality of that moral sense of oughtness that's stamped on every human heart, just the mere presence of that moral code should move every hardened skeptic to a point of intellectual openness about the existence of a supreme moral being. There simply is no other reasonable explanation."

Read Snapshot "Personal Testimony" before Question 7

Question Seven As we share some of our personal story with the group, be sure to emphasize that it ought not be a canned or rehearsed speech. An effective testimony is a heart-felt and natural expression of who God is to us and what He has done (and is doing) in our life. After group members tell their own personal testimony, talk together about how this part of their story might bless and help someone who is wondering if God exists.

Read Snapshot "Planting a Seed ... Do Versus Done" before Question 8

Question Eight This is just one example of sharing the gospel in a concise way. If your group wants to dig deeper into this topic, consider the examples presented in the *Becoming a Contagious Christian* book and curriculum.

PUTTING YOURSELF IN THE PICTURE

Challenge group members to take time in the coming week to use part or all of this application section as an opportunity for continued growth.

DOES GOD HEAR MY PRAYERS?

LUKE 18:9 – 14

INTRODUCTION

Sometimes we can slip into a prayer rut and simply go through the motions. We forget who we are speaking to and just parrot words we have memorized or that come out of our mouth with no connection to our heart. God hears our prayers, but He longs to be in a dynamic relationship with us, not hear mindless repetitions. That is the very thing Jesus warned about in the Sermon on the Mount when He said, "And when you pray, do not keep on babbling like pagans, for they think they will be heard because of their many words" (Matt. 6:7). God hears our prayers, but He longs for them to be sincere, authentic, and to the point — not lots of words, but lots of heart.

THE BIG PICTURE

Take time to read this introduction with the group. There are suggestions for how this can be done in the beginning of the leader's section.

A WIDE ANGLE VIEW

Question One No matter how long we have been a Christ follower, all of us can fall into a prayer rut. The examples in this lesson are just some of the ways we can get into a routine that looks like prayer to the casual observer but does not genuinely connect with God. The first part of this question invites group members to make general observations about how "other people" pray. Most of us have seen others fall into these shallow prayer patterns.

The goal here is not to criticize others, so help the group stay away from using names or specific situations that point to a person. The focus should be to identify that sincere people can slip into empty practices and miss the joy of real communication with God. Also, make sure you have time to discuss how

God feels about these kinds of prayers. He longs for a living and vibrant relationship with His people and this means authentic prayer really matters to God.

As you dig into the second part of the question, things get more personal and go a bit deeper. Group members are invited to tell about a pseudo-prayer pattern they can enter into. Again, the focus in not primarily to say where we have missed the mark as much as to have a good discussion about what we can do to avoid falling into empty prayer forms.

A Biblical Portrait

Read Luke 18:9–14

Question Two Jesus is teaching about prayer by telling a story, a parable. In this story Jesus paints the picture of two men praying. Both are doing the same thing, but the end results are radically different. Jesus wants us to evaluate these prayers. He wants us to analyze the story and try to figure out what is going on in the heart of the Pharisee based on the content and the tone of his prayer. He wants us to do the same with the tax collector. When we look at them, we just might see a mirror that will teach us about prayer.

I see a number of immediate lessons in this drama:

One problem in the prayer of the Pharisee is his tone of achievement. He is so thankful for how spiritual he is and that he is not like "other people." He is obsessed with what he has not done in his quest for holiness. The prayer is about . . . him!

Another issue is that the Pharisee is looking only at externals and not at his heart. This man is bragging about his outward actions. While his tendency is to fixate on what he does, God is about the heart.

The Pharisee also stumbles when he plays the comparison game. He prays with one eye open, looking at a "sinful tax collector" and measuring himself against someone else.

The tax collector is standing some distance away in a place of humility. His posture shows reverence and awareness of who God is and who he is. He actually beats his chest in a sign of fervency, humility, and contrition.

As you study this passage together, let the images and drama unfold. And let God speak to you about the posture, content, and heart of your prayers.

SHARPENING THE FOCUS

Read Snapshot "Prayer Reveals How You See God" before Question 3

Question Three The prayers of the Pharisee and the tax collector reveal a number of things about how they viewed God:

- The Pharisee has no idea God can see his heart. He really thinks God is impressed with his outer actions and good works. The tax collector, on the other hand, seems painfully aware that God sees deep inside him, and he is ready to confess his brokenness.
- The Pharisee is unaware of the burning holiness of God. He seems to think his personal righteousness is sufficient. Conversely, the tax collector stands in the holy glow of God and can't even lift his eyes due to the blinding light.
- The Pharisee sees the road to justification as being paved by his good works … a series of "Look what I did," and "Look what I refrained from doing." The tax collector comes with empty hands and a contrite heart.

Read Snapshot "Prayer Reveals How You See Yourself" before Question 5

Question Five Again the contrast is vivid and almost painful. The Pharisee clearly sees himself as better than others, as holy enough, and a pretty good person. It almost seems like he feels God is lucky to have someone like him! The tax collector, on the other hand, sees his sin, his inability to save himself, and his utter need of God. Their view of self shaped their prayers in both tone and words.

Read Snapshot "Prayer Reveals How You See Others" before Questions 7 & 8

Question Seven Once our view of God and self is established, the way we see others will follow. Because the Pharisee misunderstood God and had an inflated, unrealistic view of himself, he was primed to see others in a contorted way. He actually thought he was righteous and the tax collector was unworthy of grace. He saw himself as a gift to God and this other man as an unwanted guest in the place of prayer. The irony is that God saw these two men in exactly the opposite light. At the end of the day, the Pharisee was not justified and he left having missed the mark in prayer. The sinful and broken tax collector, on the other hand, was forgiven and loved. His honest transparency connected him to the heart of God.

Read Snapshot "Helpful Prayer Tips" before Question 9

Question Nine These are just a few ideas of creative ways to pray. The real value will come as your group talks about some of the ways they have learned to engage God in prayer. Make sure you set aside ample time at the end of the session for this. Learn from each other. If you feel your group would receive it well, you might even want to spend time praying together, using three or four of the different approaches to prayer you have talked about.

Putting Yourself in the Picture

Challenge group members to take time in the coming week to use part or all of this application section as an opportunity for continued growth.

AREN'T ALL RELIGIONS THE SAME?

ACTS 17:16−34; JOHN 14:1−7

INTRODUCTION

Our world offers a smorgasbord of religious options. How do we deal with the fact that there are so many faith expressions? How should Christians respond? Many cope with this reality by saying, "All the religious systems are really the same except for a few inconsequential differences." The problem is, this statement is grossly inaccurate. The Christian faith is not only unique and distinct from the other religions of the world, but Jesus claimed it is the only true way to God.

In this session we will look at a number of consequences we will face if the church adopts the idea that all faiths are the same. We will also discover how to embrace the uniqueness of Jesus and the teaching of the Bible in a pluralistic world.

THE BIG PICTURE

Take time to read this introduction with the group. There are suggestions for how this can be done in the beginning of the leader's section.

A WIDE ANGLE VIEW

Question One In a world with countless options and growing emphasis on relativism, many people are afraid to say that anything is true or right. Some people view choosing a religion as of no more ultimate significance than the choice of a soft drink brand. Into this world Jesus comes and claims to be the only way to the Father. Although there are many choices in life that have no ultimate right or wrong, choosing a faith is not one of them. This decision makes all the difference in this life and in eternity.

A BIBLICAL PORTRAIT

Read Acts 17:16–34 and John 14:1–7

Question Two Both Jesus and Paul faced times of intense pressure to conform. Jesus refused and it ended up taking Him to the cross. Paul refused and was publicly beaten five times! They both had the ability to articulate the faith with clarity and power. They were gracious but unrelenting in their declaration that salvation is found only in the cross of Jesus. Paul was clear that the death and resurrection of Jesus is the hinge on which all of eternity turns (1 Cor. 15). Jesus boldly claimed to be the only way to heaven (John 14:6).

Like Jesus and Paul, we live in a culture that seeks to pressure us into conforming to the conventional wisdom of our age. Like them, we can express our faith with clarity, grace, and tenacity. And, like them, we just might face some tough consequences for standing on the truth in a world that is offended by anyone who holds to absolutes.

SHARPENING THE FOCUS

Read Snapshot "All Religions Are the Same . . . This Belief Is Illogical" before Question 3

Question Three It is a strange phenomenon, but people who insist on logic in other areas of life are ready to allow totally different rules when it comes to religion. They will declare that all religions can be equally true because we are no longer operating in the realm of reason . . . this is about faith. But those who want to maintain intellectual integrity understand that all religions can't be true and many faith assertions are mutually exclusive.

The problem with affirming that all faith claims can't be true is that it means saying some people's religious convictions are . . . wrong. No one seems to want to say this. But we must. We can say it with humility and grace, but it must be said. For example:

- If salvation comes through faith in Jesus (His life, death, and resurrection) alone, then we can say that salvation does not come through religious devotion and good works.
- If there is one God — Father, Son, and Holy Spirit — then those who claim there are thousands of gods are wrong. Their belief and assertions about God are errant.
- If Jesus was God in human flesh, then those who declare that Jesus was just a great teacher or a prophet are incorrect.

There are many other examples, but the point is clear. Once we make an assertion about Jesus, salvation, or faith, we draw lines. This is why some people are so reticent to make absolute claims of faith. The dilemma for Christians is that the Bible and Jesus make absolute claims.

Read Snapshot "All Religions Are the Same ... This Belief Is an Insult to Other Religions" before Question 5

Question Five Some people think they are being generous and embracing when they claim that all religions are really the same. Such an approach works when irreligious people are chatting with other irreligious people. But it does not fly with those who understand their faith and actually believe what they profess. When we had the panel discussion at Willow Creek, the idea that each panelist was really talking about the same basic religious beliefs became absurd almost immediately. Following is one example of how different their beliefs were. (Remember, this is just the articulation of one person representing each religion, not someone trying to speak for all adherents of their faith.)

When answering the question, "Who was Jesus?" these were the answers:

Buddhism. "Jesus is a human being, but a wise and compassionate human being, who was concerned for the suffering of humanity. The Buddhist tradition would recognize Jesus. They would also recognize the Christian perspective that Jesus is the Son of God, and they would respect that." *Question:* "But not the only way?" *Answer:* "No, not the only way."

Judaism. "I would say He is the Son of God, and I would clarify that by adding in our Hebrew Bible, which belongs to the Jewish people, we read several times that God says, 'You are my servants,' and other times, 'You are my children.' So everyone here is a son or daughter of God. But as for the preeminence of Jesus over any other religion's central figure, we leave that up to anybody to decide for themselves. Because our thought is we have our Bible and our prophets, they have their Bible and their prophets, so we let it go at that." *Question:* "So, was Jesus the Messiah?" *Answer:* "No." *Question:* "Was He the Savior of the world?" *Answer:* "No." *Question:* "Is that personality still coming sometime in the future?" *Answer:* "The orthodox, traditional Jew will still look forward to the coming of the Messiah. Most Jews, though, are not orthodox. They're conservative or reform and would say it's up to us to change the world."

Islam. "The Articles of Faith in Islam [say] to believe there is one God and to believe in all the angels, and to believe in all the scripts that have been revealed by God to all the prophets and messengers, and also to believe in all the messengers and the prophets of God, which include Jesus, peace be upon him." *Question:* "Did Jesus die on the cross?" *Answer:* "In the Qur'an it says he has not been killed. He has not been crucified. It looked like it to the Romans, but he has been lifted by God and he will be coming back to guide all mankind according to Islam."

Hinduism. "At any time God can manifest himself. It's a drama. This whole world is a drama, and God created it. He created so many religions. He wanted variety for his own pleasure, and when Jesus Christ came and Christianity came about, this is God from the all-manifested state taking the form of Jesus Christ." *Question:* "So would Hindus have respect for Jesus Christ?" *Answer:* "We do have tolerance and respect for every religion. Even in India if someone believes in something, you don't tell them not to believe in it. But what you can do is nurture it. It is better to believe in something rather than to believe in nothing." *Question:* "But He (Jesus) doesn't have any special status above any of the other incarnations from God?" *Answer:* "We have reverence for all the gods, and we have tolerance for all the gods, and we nurture every one of the gods, and we tell everyone, 'Go pray to your god if you have that belief. Continue what you're doing and let it mushroom and grow.'"

Christianity. "Christianity teaches that Jesus Christ is the one and only Son of God, that He is fully human and fully God, without sin, and the only one worthy or qualified to forgive sin. And we believe that He proved that He had the ability to forgive sin, and He proved that He was God when He was resurrected."

Read Snapshot "All Religions Are the Same ... This Belief Is Contrary to the Life and Teaching of Jesus" before Question 6

Question Six Jesus was a man of peace. He was never out looking to pick a fight. But when it came to declaring the truth, he never backed off. Throughout His ministry Jesus questioned the conventional wisdom of the political and religious world. He did not embrace all religions as equally valid, nor did He introduce Himself as one of many ways to heaven. Indeed, He was emphatic that He was the only way, God in human flesh, the hope of the world, the Messiah. Take time to read the indicated passages from the Gospel of John (see the "Putting Yourself in the Picture" section, page 57) to go deeper into this topic.

Read Snapshot "All Religions Are the Same ... This Belief is Opposed to the Teaching of the Bible" before Question 7

Question Seven From the beginning of the Bible to the end, God is seeking to deliver people from false religions, pagan worship, and slavery to idols. In the history of Israel, one of their greatest sins was embracing false gods and worshiping idols. In fact, the primary measure of a good king was that he followed Yahweh only and kept the nation from idols. On the other hand, the sin that led to judgment over and over was false worship. Read the books of 1–2 Samuel, 1–2 Kings, and 1–2 Chronicles, and this theme will come up over and over again. In addition, the major and minor prophets of the Old Testament spoke against false worship and idolatry with piercing conviction.

From start to finish, the message of the Bible is uncompromising: There is one God and the way to restored relationship with Him is found through faith in Jesus. There is no hint of teaching that all world religions are the same or equally valid.

Read Snapshot "All Religions Are the Same ... This Belief Endangers People" before Question 8

Question Eight When Christians buy into the idea that it is loving to embrace all religions as equally valid, we do not do the world a favor. In an effort to be tolerant we can end up doing the most unloving thing possible: Forgetting to tell people about the one way to heaven ... Jesus. If the Bible, the prophets, and the teachings of Jesus are right, then we must let people know that Jesus is the hope of the world, the only way to a restored relationship with God. Holding to this conviction might not always be popular. It might even cause people to see us as narrow in our religious views. But Bible-believing Christians have always risked popularity for the sake of bringing the good news of Jesus to a lost world.

We can be gracious. We don't have to be mean or contentious. But we must hold to the truth if we are going to let Jesus' light shine in the world today.

PUTTING YOURSELF IN THE PICTURE

Challenge group members to take time in the coming week to use part or all of this application section as an opportunity for continued growth.

Interactions Series

Celebrating God

Discover the Truth of God's Character

Bill Hybels with Kevin and Sherry Harney

ARE YOU READY TO CELEBRATE?

A stadium full of football fans jump to their feet and cheer with deafening volume when a game-winning pass is caught. Family members gather every year to give gifts and sing choruses of Happy Birthday. Friends congregate just to have a party ... they hardly need a reason. In the Bible God instituted festivals and feasts. There is something in the human spirit that loves to rejoice, shout, and celebrate ... and God likes it that way.

We were created for celebration, and the focal point of our praise should always be God. When we get glimpses of His character, expressions of joy should spontaneously erupt. God is a refuge; He is generous and righteous, full of extravagant love toward us. The Maker of heaven and earth is relational, He guides us, and He will never leave us. It's time to discover God's character and make Him the focal point of our celebration.

Softcover: 978-0-310-28063-7

Pick up a copy at your favorite bookstore!

Interactions Series

Excellent Living

Giving God Your Best

Bill Hybels with Kevin and Sherry Harney

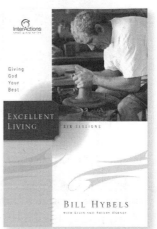

MOVE PAST "GOOD ENOUGH" TO EXCELLENT

Jesus modeled an excellent life. No person has ever lived with greater passion and love. When it was time to go to the cross, Jesus walked the hill of Calvary with excellent compassion and grace. Those who follow in the steps of Jesus hear the invitation to be like Him and embrace the joy of excellent living.

What does it look like when we seek to give God our best? It means aligning every part of our lives with His will. It means dreaming about a future that will be shaped by the holy hands of God. No part of our journey is outside of His view and touch. In the power of Jesus we can live excellent lives on every level: spiritually, morally, relationally, financially, directionally, and eternally. This kind of life honors God and leads to the greatest joy possible.

Softcover: 978-0-310-28064-4

Pick up a copy at your favorite bookstore!

Interactions Series

Influence

Maximizing Your Impact for God

Bill Hybels with Kevin and Sherry Harney

YOUR LIFE MEANS MORE THAN YOU KNOW

God wants you to be a world changer ... starting right where you are today. Your acts of service, words of truth, love for God, care for people, and all you do each day can have a transformational impact on the people around you. In a world filled with darkness and discouragement, the light of heaven can shine through you.

Jesus was the most influential person in human history. He brought joy to the sorrowful, hope to the broken, purpose to the wandering, and forgiveness to all who would receive Him. The ministry of Jesus continues today. One way the Savior brings His world-changing message to this generation is through you and me.

It's time for us to let the Holy Spirit flow freely. It's time to influence the world with the love of Jesus. It's time to maximize our impact for God!

Softcover: 978-0-310-28066-8

Pick up a copy at your favorite bookstore!

ReGroup™

Training Groups to Be Groups

Henry Cloud, Bill Donahue, and *John Townsend*

Whether you're a new or seasoned group leader, or whether your group is well-established or just getting started, the *ReGroup*™ small group DVD and participant's guide will lead you and your group together to a remarkable new closeness and effectiveness. Designed to foster healthy group interaction and facilitate maximum growth, this innovative approach equips both group leaders and members with essential skills and values for creating and sustaining truly life-changing small groups. Created by three group life experts, the two DVDs in this kit include:

- Four sixty-minute sessions on the foundations of small groups that include teaching by the authors, creative segments, and activities and discussion time
- Thirteen five-minute coaching segments on topics such as active listening, personal sharing, giving and receiving feedback, prayer, calling out the best in others, and more

A participant's guide is sold separately.

DVD: 978-0-310-27783-5
Participant's Guide: 978-0-310-27785-9

Pick up a copy at your favorite bookstore!

Share Your Thoughts

With the Author: Your comments will be forwarded to the author when you send them to *zauthor@zondervan.com*.

With Zondervan: Submit your review of this book by writing to *zreview@zondervan.com*.

Free Online Resources at
www.zondervan.com

Zondervan AuthorTracker: Be notified whenever your favorite authors publish new books, go on tour, or post an update about what's happening in their lives at www.zondervan.com/authortracker.

Daily Bible Verses and Devotions: Enrich your life with daily Bible verses or devotions that help you start every morning focused on God. Visit www.zondervan.com/newsletters.

Free Email Publications: Sign up for newsletters on Christian living, academic resources, church ministry, fiction, children's resources, and more. Visit www.zondervan.com/newsletters.

Zondervan Bible Search: Find and compare Bible passages in a variety of translations at www.zondervanbiblesearch.com.

Other Benefits: Register yourself to receive online benefits like coupons and special offers, or to participate in research.

ZONDERVAN®

ZONDERVAN.com/
AUTHORTRACKER
follow your favorite authors